Bitter Freedom

Bitter Freedom

William Stone's Record of Service in the Freedmen's Bureau

EDITED BY
Suzanne Stone Johnson and Robert Allison Johnson

INTRODUCTION BY Lou Falkner Williams

THE UNIVERSITY OF SOUTH CAROLINA PRESS

Published by the University of South Carolina Press
Columbia, South Carolina 29208

www.sc.edu/uscpress

Manufactured in the United States of America

17 16 15 14 13 12 11 10 09 08 10 9 8 7 6 5 4 3 2 1

Library of Congress Cataloging-in-Publication Data

Stone, William, 1842–1897.
Bitter freedom : William Stone's record of service in the Freedmen's Bureau / edited by Suzanne Stone Johnson and Robert Allison Johnson ; introduction by Lou Falkner Williams.
p. cm.
Includes bibliographical references and index.
ISBN 978-1-57003-766-5 (cloth : alk. paper)
1. Reconstruction (U.S. history, 1865–1877)—South Carolina. 2. United States. Bureau of Refugees, Freedmen, and Abandoned Lands. 3. Freedmen—South Carolina—History—19th century. 4. South Carolina—Social conditions—19th century. 5. South Carolina—Race relations—History—19th century. 6. Edgefield County (S.C.)—Social conditions—19th century. 7. Edgefield County (S.C.)—Race relations—History—19th century. 8. Stone, William, 1842–1897. 9. United States. Bureau of Refugees, Freedmen, and Abandoned Lands—Officials and employees—Biography. I. Johnson, Suzanne Stone, 1929– II. Johnson, Robert, 1928– III. Title.
F274.S84 2008
973.7'14—dc22

2008018752

This book was printed on Glatfelter Natures, a recycled paper with 30 percent postconsumer waste content.

Contents

Illustrations

Preface

Why should we care about the lives of those who preceded us on this earth? Their lives are done with. We live in the present—not the past. The answer, of course, is that our ancestors *made* the world in which *we* now live.

As David McCullough said in an address delivered at a recent Hillsdale College seminar,

> Family, teachers, friends, rivals, competitors—they've all shaped us. And so too have people we've never met, never known, because they lived long before us. They have shaped us too—the people who composed the symphonies that move us, the painters, the poets, those who have written the great literature in our language. . . .
>
> How can we not want to know about the people who made it possible for us to live as we live, to have the freedoms we have, to be citizens of this greatest of countries in all time? It's not just a birthright, it is something that others struggled for, strived for, often suffered for, often were defeated for and died for, for us, for the next generation.[1]

How very different our lives today would be had it not been for the lives and actions of such heroic figures as Winston Churchill, Thomas Jefferson, and Abraham Lincoln, as well as millions of lesser-known achievers, including my great-grandfather William Stone. He first came to the South to fight for the Union during the Civil War and stayed when the fighting ended to take part in the work of reconstruction. In late 1868 William Stone, after being employed for nearly three years as an agent of the Bureau of Refugees, Freedmen, and Abandoned Lands (the Freedmen's Bureau), sat down at his desk and penned 190 pages of recollections of that incredible postwar experience. For more than a century those pages languished in the archives of his descendants. Thanks to the University of South Carolina Press and his great-grandchildren (my cousins

Dorothy S. Franks and W. Wallace Stone, my sister Nancy S. Wilson, and me, Suzanne S. Johnson), this remarkable slice of history is available to anyone interested in how the modern South came to be.

It has been more than four generations since the great American Civil War ended and the victorious North embarked on a bold social and political experiment to "reconstruct" the defeated South. That experiment, which was largely abandoned in 1877, was not only a failure in its attempt to transform the culture of the South into a Republican-dominated version of the North, but it also exacerbated sectional resentments that still occasionally emerge in our national culture. Even today Northerners who relocate to the more rural parts of the Deep South can confirm that these resentments are at times palpable.

Much of Major Stone's report is, to a person interested in the past, a fascinating view of the postwar South—its poverty, its political shenanigans, its racial hatred, the animosity of its white population toward Yankees—all experienced by a man in the thick of it. As Stone explains, nearly all of the postwar assistance given to the impoverished South came through voluntary contributions from charitable organizations in the North. The federal government, led by Radical Republicans, focused on social revolution rather than restoration. A student of recent history might well contrast Southern Reconstruction with the American aid given through the Marshall Plan to a devastated Germany after World War II. As a result of that assistance, a reconstructed Germany became one of our staunchest allies.

We hope that William Stone would have been proud of his progeny. We, his descendants, know that we are proud of him and the significant contribution he made to our world, not only through his accomplishments but also of the sense of history that led him to record his experiences at a critical point in the life of our nation. Readers interested in a detailed, personal account of William Stone's entire life are invited to read *This Violent Land,* written by my husband, Robert Johnson, and published in 2007 by Bright Mountain Books of Fairview, North Carolina.

Reaching back in time to touch the lives of our ancestors is never easy. William Stone, through his carefully maintained journals and diaries, opened the door for us. We are grateful to him for his foresight.

SUZANNE STONE JOHNSON

Note

1. David McCullough, "Knowing History and Knowing Who We Are," *Imprimis,* April 2005, http://www.hillsdale.edu/news/imprimis/archive/issue.asp?year=2005&month=04 (accessed January 30, 2008). Reprinted by permission from *Imprimis*, the national speech digest of Hillsdale College.

Introduction

> *I know how you feel while you are at this wearisome and almost thankless work. I sometimes feel myself as if my brain were never to find rest but to be always in a strain. I suppose a change will come by and by. Were it not that this is so interesting a period of our history, I should almost be inclined to let all this work go by the board for the sake of being among civilized beings again. As it is, I am deeply interested in this great social and political problem we are working out and look to the future full of hope and confidence.*
>
> William Stone to Erastus Everson, August 18, 1869

Bitter Freedom: William Stone's Record of Service in the Freedmen's Bureau provides an extraordinary opportunity to view the condition of South Carolina at the end of the Civil War and beginning of Reconstruction through the eyes of a young Freedmen's Bureau agent who was eager to do his part to reconstruct the Union. Stone was an exceptionally dedicated and bright young United States Army officer—only twenty-three when he arrived in South Carolina—who was curious about everything and steadfast in his determination to commit his thoughts to paper. Idealistic and hopeful regarding the opportunity to prepare the former slaves for the privileges and responsibilities of citizenship, Stone learned quickly that a "wearisome and almost thankless" task lay before the victorious Yankees as they sought to remake the South in the "free soil" image of the North. The image of the Yankee carpetbagger as an intruder bent on enriching himself at any cost to white Southerners has long been discredited, but Stone's account sheds new light on the Republican national government's efforts to reconstruct the rebel states before so many things went wrong.[1]

Neither an official government record nor a diary, Stone's record of his service in the Freedmen's Bureau is perhaps best understood as his personal summary of all that he saw and accomplished as a Freedmen's Bureau agent in South Carolina. Stone compiled the record from official records he was required to keep, from journals that have not been preserved, and from his recollections.[2] The record is remarkable for its astute political and economic analysis, its insight regarding the effects of slavery on every aspect of Southern life, and its strong sense of the historical importance of what the United States government hoped to accomplish in South Carolina. The document is divided into three parts. Part 1 begins with Stone's appointment to the Freedmen's Bureau and his initial impressions of the state. It reviews Stone's efforts to improve the lives of the former slaves, especially his oversight of labor contracts and his determination to establish black schools. Stone's assessments of the political situation and the effects of slavery on the economy and morals of both races are perhaps the most important material here. Part 2 recounts Stone's experience in Edgefield County, of which Aiken was then a part. Here, too, he discusses his work with the freedmen's schools and the teachers who ran them. Surprisingly, however, he does not discuss the Schofield School, the one with which he was most intimately connected. Stone's emphasis and interest in part 2 shift to politics and law enforcement in Edgefield, which had a well-deserved reputation for being the most violent county in the state. Stone regarded his experience as a judge on the provost court as his most important contribution to federal Reconstruction efforts. As in part 1, Stone's astute analysis of Reconstruction politics and the moral effects of slavery on the entire population is the most important aspect of this section. Part 3 is remarkable primarily for Stone's ideas regarding the continued existence of the Freedmen's Bureau. He was willing—even eager—to do away with the bureau. "Now that the colored men have been endowed with the same political and civil rights as the whites," he wrote, "it is a question whether they ought longer to be subjects for special legislation."[3] It was early in the process of Reconstruction and William Stone, like the majority of Northerners, did not understand that respect for constitutional amendments and federal law paled in comparison with the South's devotion to its ancient traditions. He would learn, soon enough, that ongoing federal protection was necessary if a rule of law strong enough to protect black Americans was to survive.

Under the authority of the War Department, Congress established the Bureau of Refugees, Freedmen, and Abandoned Lands in March 1865 to oversee the transition from slavery to freedom for the former slaves. It was the duty of the Freedmen's Bureau to coordinate federal relief efforts, to manage "all subjects relating to refugees and freedmen from the rebel states," and to "set apart for the use of loyal refugees and freedmen" the lands that had been abandoned or confiscated during the war. Thus it seemed initially that the national government would actually provide land to make independent farmers of the former slaves. By the time William Stone arrived in Anderson, South Carolina, in March 1866, however, President Andrew Johnson's wholesale pardon policy had returned most of the so-called abandoned lands to the previous owners, robbing blacks of their dreams of land ownership and self-sufficiency. Hence Stone's efforts on behalf of the freed people of South Carolina—like those of bureau agents throughout the South—were concentrated primarily in four other important areas: providing emergency relief, overseeing labor contract negotiations between land owners and black agricultural workers, founding schools and overseeing the education of the freed people, and protecting the legal rights of black Southerners.[4]

William Stone's background had uniquely qualified him for the work of Reconstruction. Born in 1842 in East Machias, Maine, Stone was the son of a prominent New England cleric, Thomas Treadwell Stone, a writer and intellectual, one of the lesser-known of Bronson Alcott's Transcendentalist circle, who was best known for his radical abolitionist views. As early as the 1830s Thomas Stone was exhorting his congregation that slavery was a *national* problem. Americans had no right to boast of their freedom and equality while millions of people who were also formed in God's image were held in bondage. It was the duty of all Christians, according to the senior Stone, "to do our utmost in resisting [slavery], through the Spirit of Christ." Thomas Stone was removed from his Congregational pulpit in Maine for his radical stand against slavery and—according to Stone family tradition—for serving communion to a black man. Thomas went on to serve as pastor of the First Church Congregational in Salem, Massachusetts, where his outspoken abolitionist sentiments soon earned him severe censure from the parishioners despite that state's reputation as the most abolitionist of all states. Thomas promptly converted to Unitarianism.[5] As a Unitarian, his son noted proudly, Thomas had "fully realized the delight of a broad and liberal faith especially coming into it as he did from the old orthodox notions of our Puritan fathers . . . who had too much of the old and too little of the New Testament in them." In the "radical wing of Unitarianism," Thomas Stone found a church with social views broad enough to accommodate his outspoken abolitionism.[6] Settling his family in the small town of Bolton, Massachusetts, Thomas ministered to the local Unitarian church while keeping up his abolitionist work on the New England lecture circuit. Clearly his son William had lived with radical abolitionist views his entire life. Unfortunately, however, Thomas Stone's vocation did not pay enough to support his family. The family farm in Bolton had to make up the difference.

William Stone's values were shaped as much by the rigors of farm life in New England as by his father's abolitionist principles. He began a diary at age fifteen, in which he wrote almost every day until he left home to join the Union army in 1861. The entries are generally short, almost inevitably about the weather, and not particularly reflective. Nevertheless the diaries provide sound information about the young man's life and character, including his personal views against slavery. As a farm kid, William was accustomed to hard work in rhythm with the changing seasons. His diaries record sowing and harvesting, hoeing the garden, and above all rising early to cut wood before school. Because his two older brothers were away in college, William was often expected to bear the brunt of the farmwork, which he did industriously and without complaint. He attended a local school and clearly enjoyed the learning process. He attended "meeting" at his father's church every Sunday morning and often visited other local churches on Sunday afternoons. Perhaps reflecting the Unitarian faith in which he had been brought up, William took an intense dislike to the local Baptist minister, noting that he "brought up some of the meanest arguments" that the young Stone had ever heard.[7]

William Stone enjoyed visiting with family and friends, skating and sledding in the winter, swimming in the summer, taking long walks in the country, reading aloud or playing games with family and friends, and playing the fiddle. He attended dancing school and an occasional singing school. He was an avid and generally successful member of the local debate team. Through debate he explored such timely topics as immediate emancipation of the slaves and women's suffrage. He supported the local lyceum and attended concerts. For a small rural town, Bolton offered many opportunities for educational and cultural refinement. William Stone was no rube. Thus it is little wonder that he considered most of the small towns in South Carolina unworthy of being called towns.[8]

Stone's boyhood diary also demonstrates his personal commitment to the antislavery movement and his emerging dedication to Republican Party principles. Too young to vote in the 1860 presidential election, William Stone nevertheless did everything in his power to get out the vote for

Lincoln and the Republican Party. Beginning in early September, he put up posters for Republican meetings, fashioned letters for Lincoln flags, filled torches for a nighttime demonstration, attended Republican meetings regularly, and helped to found a Lincoln and Hamlin Club. On election day he hung around the polls and waited anxiously for the returns. His journal noted the precise results with obvious satisfaction: 151 votes for Lincoln, a strong majority in his small town.[9]

Stone conveyed his pleasure with the election results in a letter to his father. He was proud of his home state, which had not only supported Lincoln but also elected a Republican governor and six congressmen "chosen solely on the ground of his [*sic*] opposition to slavery." "Antislavery means something here," he boasted. Judging Lincoln to be a man of "firmness, honesty, and a resolute will," Stone predicted that the president-elect could handle "those southern fire-eaters." As for South Carolina's "Declaration of Independence," it was a "silly, ridiculous piece of nonsense" in William's mind. Noting that secession was the work of politicians eager to tear the Union apart, William predicted optimistically that the people of South Carolina would come to their senses and recognize the shame involved in leaving the Union.[10] Stone had accurately predicted Lincoln's resolve, but grossly underestimated the determination of South Carolina and the other Southern states.

South Carolina withdrew from the Union almost immediately after Lincoln's election in 1860. North and South had become increasingly alienated throughout the antebellum period. Compromises between the sections delayed the break but could not resolve the moral issue at the core of the sectional conflict. Lincoln's Republican Party "free soil" platform stated clearly that no further expansion of slavery into the western territories would be allowed. Without further expansion of slavery, the South understood, the North would *eventually* have enough votes to free the slaves by constitutional amendment. Thus white South Carolinians had good reason to fear the approaching end of slavery when an all Northern, antislavery Republican party had elected Lincoln without his name even appearing on the ballot in most of the Southern states.[11]

When Lincoln called for troops in 1861, William enlisted with friends and family members from his hometown. These young men from Bolton were a part of the Nineteenth Massachusetts Infantry Regiment, one of those units that participated in almost every important battle on the eastern front. William kept a journal throughout the war, writing in it almost every day. Like so many Civil War diaries, Stone's diary records the monotony of camp life, the heat, the cold, the mud he experienced on marches, and the rare pleasure of a decent meal. He kept up his correspondence with many friends and family members back home. And he read numerous books with a much more intellectual bent than one would expect of a foot soldier.[12]

Throughout the difficult trials of Union defeat in battle after battle, William maintained his optimism that the Union would eventually prevail. William experienced hard fighting for the first time on June 25, 1862, in the Seven Days' Battle. He recorded the names of his friends who had died or had "narrow escapes" and noted with relief that he had "been spared" and that the men fought "very well seeing it was the first time they were ever engaged."[13] At Antietam, on the bloodiest day of the entire war, September 17, 1862, the Nineteenth suffered heavy casualties, with as many as half the men dead or wounded, and Stone himself was severely wounded, the nerves of his right arm almost completely destroyed. Fortunately, perhaps, Stone was still convalescing at home in Bolton when his regiment again took heavy casualties at Fredericksburg in the assault on Marye's Heights. As the nation's confidence lagged, Stone insisted in a letter meant for publication that the Union soldiers were confident and determined to keep up the fight as long as it should take. He did not generally discuss the meaning of the war in his diary; however, it is clear that he knew exactly why he was fighting. It was the "accursed system of slavery," he noted after attending a black prayer meeting, "which the success of our arms is to destroy and root out forever. To be able to fight for such a cause, the cause of freedom and humanity is worth any sacrifice."[14] Having been commissioned a second lieutenant shortly after Antietam, Stone returned to the field in time to lead a company in combat at Chancellorsville.[15]

The Battle of Gettysburg turned the tide of the war for the Union army and ended William Stone's combat experience. On the morning of July 2, 1863, with his company already formed in line for battle, he took time to write that the entire Army of the Potomac was concentrated at Gettysburg, and "it seems as if we ought to whip the rebels." Stone was wounded a third time on the second day of Gettysburg, receiving a head wound that sent him to hospital in the rear. The Nineteenth Massachusetts fought hard and again suffered dreadfully on July 3. Stone noted with pride that the men had "behaved admirably" and recorded the casualties among the officers and men he knew. This time Stone's optimism was well founded; after Gettysburg and the fall of Vicksburg, both on Independence Day 1863, the Union army was well on its way to victory. William Stone returned to Bolton for a short convalescent leave, then rejoined his company briefly before he was transferred to the Invalid Corps and a desk job in Philadelphia for the remainder of the war.[16] He was assigned to the Freedmen's Bureau in South Carolina in March 1866, just under a year after Appomattox, probably because of his whole-hearted commitment to black rights.

As a Freedmen's Bureau agent, William Stone paid careful attention to everything in his path. Much of the report reads like a travel narrative of South Carolina after the war. He reports on the sorry condition of the roads and bridges, the lack of transportation, the devastation left behind by Sherman's troops, and the difficulty of rebuilding with so little capital available. While Stone was sympathetic toward Southerners who had lost everything to Sherman's march, he believed nevertheless that it may have been just.[17] Stone entertained no doubt that the industrious Yankees would have cleared away the ruins and started to rebuild sooner than Southerners had managed to do.

Stone's perceptions of South Carolina were perhaps typical of most New Englanders. By the 1850s, according to historian Eric Foner, Northern society had developed the view that the Southern states were inferior. Whereas Northerners were progressive, industrious, entrepreneurial, thrifty, and sober, Southerners—lacking a strong Protestant work ethic and accustomed to a slave society and economy—were backward, indolent, and—in William Stone's report—downright shiftless. "To those with visions of a steadily growing nation," according to Foner, "slavery was an intolerable hindrance to national achievement." Yankees defined their own economic success in terms of fee-simple land ownership, free labor, and "their own hard work."[18] In the cotton South, however, land ownership was less important than property in human chattel. The average slave owner had around two-thirds of his wealth tied up in slave labor. Because slaves were movable personal property, cotton planters tended to exhaust the land and move on. Hence, the historian Gavin Wright argues, slave owners, generally speaking, had little attachment to place and therefore little interest in town building or industrial development.[19]

The Republican Party emerged in the 1850s as an all Northern, antislavery, free soil party, completely opposed to any further extension of slavery into the western territories. Republican Party "free labor" ideology insisted that American prosperity depended upon the right of independent laborers to choose their own vocations and enjoy the fruits of their labor.[20] For the most radical Republicans, emancipation was only the first step toward citizenship and equal rights for African Americans. It is important to note, however, that the Radicals were never a majority of the Republican Party.

William Stone was a *Radical* Republican who personified the so-called Yankee virtues: industriousness, thrift, orderliness, and sobriety. Throughout the report he kept a running commentary on the many ways in which —at least in Stone's mind—South Carolina failed to live up to the North's example. Stone was accustomed to careful agricultural practices designed to coax the best possible yield from the cold New England soil. Unlike New England, South Carolina was blessed with fertile lands and mild climate, yet the people had failed to be good stewards of the land. Stone's thrifty New England mind could not fathom agricultural practices that used up the land and moved on rather than bothering to do something as simple as applying manure. Even where the crops looked good, "thousands of acres of good land are lying idle waiting for someone to cultivate and improve them." "Under a free labor system," Stone predicted, "more careful cultivation and improved implements must be adopted."[21]

Stone's New England values clearly dictated his response to the South's economic system. He commented on each district's natural resources and failure to exploit them throughout the report.[22] His Yankee standards provoked a similar reaction to some of the Southern social customs he observed. Regarding drunkenness as a serious failure of character, he was not amused that many Southerners not only drank too much but also regarded drunkenness as "an amiable weakness of trifling moment."[23] The problem with South Carolina, in short, was that it was so unlike New England.

Stone's abolitionist background had predisposed him to despise the effects of slavery, and South Carolina provided "ample proof of the severest charges" brought against the South's "peculiar institution." Stone blamed the "blighting influence" of slavery for the backwardness he found all around him. Southerners had invested their money first and foremost in slave labor. The capitalization of labor meant that slave owners did not have to depend on their crops for their livelihood. Their wealth increased automatically as the slave population increased.[24] It is difficult to discern how *literally* Stone meant his written accusation of "slave breeding," which may have been as much a reflection of his abolitionist background as his experience in South Carolina. As Stone noted, the interstate slave trade moved surplus slaves from Virginia and the Carolinas to the lower South. The separation of slave families was rampant. Slave women, moreover, were valued primarily for their "breeding" capacity. Many owners provided special privileges—food, clothing, time off work—as incentives for child bearing. The slave narratives even reveal a few masters who forced sexual intercourse between slaves, and more who insisted that slaves marry against their will. Nevertheless most masters allowed their slaves the liberty to choose their own mates. Many slaveholders allowed their slaves to marry off the plantation and provided weekend passes for spousal visits. Others purchased the slave wife or husband to accommodate the wishes of their laborers. In turn the pressure for slave women to have children at regular intervals was intense. Between these "rewards and punishments," Deborah Gray White argues, "slaveholders had no need for 'breeding farms' per se, and there is little evidence that such existed." It is clear, however, that all masters hoped to profit from a good harvest of slave children.[25]

Stone reserved his bitterest criticism of slavery for its effects on religion and morality. In his opinion slavery had corrupted Christianity and compromised the sanctity of marriage. Southerners of both races were sincere in their Christian beliefs, Stone observed, but neither blacks nor whites had embraced the moral precepts that should have accompanied marriage. Because masters had separated slave spouses for "superficial reasons," the former slaves were "careless of the marriage relation."[26] Masters cheated their laborers of "personal freedom and the fruits of their labors." The slaves responded by preferring "idleness to work." Lacking a strong Yankee work ethic, both races suffered during Reconstruction. Above all, Stone noted the hypocrisy of a Christianity in which slaves were "'converted' by the same instrumentalities, baptized in the same manner, preached to as frequently, . . . received the sacrament from the same vessels," and were buried with the same religious rites, yet which refused to recognize that holding fellow human beings in bondage was a sin.[27]

Stone's abolitionist background had prepared him ideologically for his new responsibilities as a Freedmen's Bureau agent, but neither William Stone nor the Freedmen's Bureau that he represented were welcome in Reconstruction South Carolina. Defeat on the battlefield had not reconciled white Southerners to the end of slavery; racial values nourished through centuries of slavery would not change overnight. As far as most white South Carolinians were concerned, slavery was the appropriate position for blacks, who were innately, immutably inferior to whites. Thus the efforts of Freedmen's Bureau agents like William Stone to ease racial tensions and protect the rights of African Americans were considered intolerable meddling with the perceived natural order of the races.

The United States faced in 1865 the enormous difficulty of determining exactly what freedom would mean for the four million former slaves. Would freedom bring land, opportunity, and political equality as the former slaves and many Northerners hoped? If Yankee free labor ideology—through which all people had access to opportunity—was to succeed in the South, blacks needed land and homes of their own. White Southerners, however, were accustomed to a society where even free blacks' lives were circumscribed in numerous ways, including restrictions on job opportunities, curfews, and proscriptions about testifying against white people. When white Southerners contemplated the meaning of freedom for the emancipated slaves, they generally understood it as little more than the mere absence of slavery. Emancipation, in Southern terms, did not mean that the former slaves would enjoy the same rights as white people. Southern whites fully expected to maintain a system as much like slavery as possible.

The task of easing the transition from slavery to freedom fell to the Freedmen's Bureau agents across the South. White Southerners who expected to manage race relations according to their own traditions and to make labor arrangements without the interference of "meddling Yankees" naturally resented the bureau. The work of the Freedmen's Bureau agent was difficult, demanding, and often downright dangerous. Manpower was always short. Thus it was completely impossible for the agents to attend to the needs of all the freed people in their districts. Perceived as the enemy, Freedmen's Bureau agents got little respect from white South Carolinians. The endless paperwork and official reports—all handwritten—only added to the problems. Burnout and loneliness were serious problems.[28]

Adding to the burdens of the Freedmen's Bureau agents, the federal government was deeply divided between Lincoln's successor, President Andrew Johnson, who hoped to restore the rebel states to the Union as quickly and painlessly as possible, and a Republican Congress set on remaking the

South in the free soil image of the North. Without consulting Congress, Johnson instituted a very lenient plan of reconstruction that included thousands of presidential pardons for former Confederate officials. When the Thirty-ninth Congress met in December 1865, the Republican majority refused to seat the Southern delegates elected under Johnson's plan, then proceeded to pass more stringent Reconstruction measures than it might have done if the South had displayed any signs of repentance. Recognizing the necessity of protecting the rights of former slaves, Republicans passed a law extending the life of the Freedmen's Bureau and granting it additional power to create courts to protect the legal rights of blacks in states where they were not allowed to testify in court or serve on juries. Johnson promptly vetoed the bill, his bullheadedness pushing Congress toward even stricter Reconstruction measures.

Congress passed thereafter a series of laws and constitutional amendments designed to provide civil and political rights for the nation's four million former slaves. The Civil Rights Act of 1866 gave blacks basic civil rights: the right to sign a contract, the right to sue or be sued in court, the right to marry legally, and the right to legal guardianship of their own children. The law also empowered the federal government to intervene when state courts did not protect black rights. The Fourteenth Amendment provided citizenship for the former slaves and attempted, under the equal protection clause, the privileges and immunities clause, and the due process clause, to provide for blacks the same rights that white people enjoyed.

With the Military Reconstruction Act of 1867, Congress invalidated Johnson's efforts and took control of Reconstruction. The bill divided the Southern states—excepting Tennessee, which had already been readmitted to the Union—into five military districts, each governed by a military governor. Readmission to the Union required enfranchisement of black men, ratification of the Thirteenth and Fourteenth Amendments, and a new state constitution. Once these requirements were completed, the state could elect a government and be readmitted to the Union. Congressional Reconstruction was clearly a more stringent policy than Johnson wanted, but it is important to note that the ex-Confederates—technically traitors to the Union—were neither punished for treason nor permanently disqualified from political participation. Moreover they retained property rights without fear of confiscation or redistribution of their land. Most white Southerners, nevertheless, bitterly resented federal Reconstruction policy and considered the Republican state governments founded under congressional policy completely unconstitutional. Black participation in state political affairs at a time when many whites were unable to vote offended whites and increased their determination to retake their "rightful" authority at the first opportunity. Recognizing Southern intransigence, Congress passed the Fifteenth Amendment, the last of the Reconstruction amendments, which provided constitutional authority for black voting rights and forbade states to deprive citizens of the vote because of race, color, or previous condition of servitude. White South Carolinians, unfortunately, never recognized the authority of federal law or the state's Republican government to protect the newly established rights of black citizens. Political violence against both black and white Republicans became a mainstay of Reconstruction era South Carolina.[29]

As Congress passed successively more stringent Reconstruction measures, the authority and responsibilities of the Freedmen's Bureau agents shifted also. The most immediate needs in Anderson County when William Stone arrived in 1866 were food, clothing, and medical attention. Agents throughout the state provided food enough to save thousands of destitute South Carolinians from starving in the early postbellum period. Agents distributed clothing provided by the army's quartermaster general and by Northern benevolent societies. They employed doctors to care for the sick and supplied free transportation to return displaced people to their homes. Just when the bureau expected to cut back on the humanitarian aid, crops failed in 1866; South Carolina was faced with hunger and destitution. Bureau agents were forced—against their notions that people should take care of themselves—to continue feeding the hungry.[30]

Bureau regulations called for "great discrimination" and "strict accountability" in determining who would receive the government rations. The idea was to relieve the immediate hardship while encouraging good Yankee habits of frugality and self-reliance for the long term.[31] William Stone's reflections on this humanitarian effort demonstrate both a real need for government aid and the difficulty of determining those who were actually destitute. Stone despised the "worthless vagabonds both white and black who always begged rather than steal and stole rather than work," but admitted it was a time of "universal distress." Stone fed people of every stripe, from "penniless aristocrats" to "broken down slaves." He struggled nevertheless with the necessity of feeding able-bodied Americans who should have been able to support themselves. Such a thing would not have been necessary, he noted, "at the North where labor is diversified." Because the South had depended almost entirely on agriculture, the 1866 famine left almost everyone in trouble. Stone complained justifiably that the Freedmen's Bureau had never received "due credit" for its relief efforts among the people of South Carolina. Whites willingly took what they could get from the government yet refused to demonstrate any gratitude.[32]

The Freedmen's Bureau is best remembered for its oversight of labor contracts between land owners and laborers as the South made the difficult transition from slavery to a free labor system. The idea was to develop a labor policy that would restore order and function smoothly. Bureau officials mediated difficulties between land owners who expected to treat their workers like slaves and former slaves who had yet to learn steady, reliable work habits as free laborers. Once the contracts were signed, it was up to the bureau's agents to insist on compliance from both sides. Blacks generally contracted to farm on "shares," a greater or lesser share depending on the area in which they lived and whether or not they were to be furnished with tools and provisions. Historians have faulted Freedmen's Bureau agents for favoring the planter class—at the expense of the freedmen's needs—in their haste to establish a contract labor system and impose order across the South. The historian LaWanda Cox suggests, however, that this interpretation is grounded too much in the complaints of white Southerners who were naturally resentful of the federal government's intervention. The bureau did its best, she argues, to obtain officers who were "sympathetic in their attitude toward the Negroes and also discreet and judicious" in dealing with both races.[33] Clearly some bureau agents fell far short of that goal, but many did not. William Stone's careful oversight of labor contracts demonstrates his personal integrity and his determination to do his best for both laborers and land owners. Stone immediately disapproved, for example, owners who paid the "merest pittance" and those who attempted to treat their workers "just as they had done while they were slaves"—providing food and clothing but no wages. By the end of the summer, Stone reported, "most of the men were convinced of the necessity of paying good wages to their hands." He kept a copy of each contract in the office for reference when either side complained of contract violation.[34]

Like Freedmen's Bureau agents across the South, Stone worked hard to establish schools for the former slaves. He faced two enormous obstacles in this endeavor: lack of money and hostility from the white community. Stone established a school at Anderson immediately after his arrival there. The local whites did not object, and a local man even agreed to teach. When the Freedman's Union Commission agreed to provide the teacher's salary, the project was set—despite threats from local whites—and classes began. Establishing schools in other areas, however, proved more difficult. Stone reported numerous problems: a black minister who had been active in the educational effort was brutally murdered on the way home from a revival meeting, military protection was necessary to protect the teacher at Belton, a Massachusetts Methodist minister who started a school at Aiken was forced out of town. When a teacher from Columbia left Aiken after only three weeks, Stone persuaded his sister Martha to take charge of the Aiken school for the remainder of the school year. His willingness to subject his own sister to the disapproval and hatred of the local whites demonstrates his complete dedication to black education.[35]

In 1868 two young Quaker educators, who would prove more successful in the long run, arrived in Aiken. Both Martha Schofield and Mary Taylor had taught previously in freedmen's schools in Mount Pleasant, South Carolina, near Charleston. Schofield had fallen seriously ill with the "seasonal fever" and returned to her home in Pennsylvania for the summer. After she recovered, she decided to relocate in Aiken, where the climate was healthier. These women established one of the most successful black schools in the entire South, the Schofield Industrial and Normal School, which is today a part of the public school system in Aiken. Schofield and Taylor were generally ostracized by Southern whites who opposed the school, because they feared the Yankee teachers were imparting dangerous notions of social equality along with reading and writing. According to Schofield's biographer, William Stone immediately became their protector, friend, and frequent caller. Schofield was sorely disappointed to lose her colleague when Mary Taylor left the school to marry William Stone in 1869.[36]

Unfortunately the Freedmen's Bureau did not have the money to pay the teachers and support the schools they started. Northern missionary efforts and the freed people themselves were left to shoulder the financial burden. In Stone's mind, "No missionary enterprise of this generation has promised or accomplished so great results as this movement for raising up and educating the emancipated blacks of the South." Nevertheless it would take a great deal more time and effort "to raise them to the full dignity of manhood and womanhood."[37]

Stone's ideas regarding education were extremely radical—even for a Massachusetts Republican. According to Stone, black children worked much harder than poor whites to learn and threatened to surpass them if the "poor whites of the South do not show soon such a desire for acquiring knowledge as is manifested by the colored people." Technically the freedmen's schools were open to white children as well as black. Stone did not know of any whites who had taken advantage of the opportunity, but he nevertheless considered it a good idea for them to attend school together. He admitted, however, that it was "no small task at the North" to overcome resistance to mixed schools, and "has not yet been accomplished there."[38]

As important as Stone believed black education to be, he considered his efforts to protect the legal rights of blacks the most important work he contributed to the Reconstruction effort. Because Edgefield County was rampant with violence against blacks, the army established a provost court there. As the ranking officer of the three-man court, Stone presided over the trials. He also served as judge advocate if the defendant lacked legal counsel. This court, Stone noted, "met frequently," sentenced whites for crimes against blacks, "gave summary judgements," and enforced prompt disposition. Although Edgefield had been known as a "turbulent area" since colonial times, Stone boasted that crimes "committed against negroes . . . ceased almost entirely."[39] Sadly, Edgefield would revert to its violent tradition when the military court closed and the state was readmitted to the Union in 1868. African Americans—despite their newly recognized right to testify against white people and serve on juries—simply could not depend on justice in the state court system.

Stone's experience on the provost court clearly steered him in the direction of the legal career that he chose when he resigned his commission in 1870. Recognizing the bureau's role in settling disputes for the freedmen, Stone had purchased his first law book, a copy of Blackstone, en route to his first bureau assignment. Now he read law in his spare time to make up for his deficits as an officer of the court. Interestingly, Stone praised the members of the Edgefield bar—despite obvious differences in political opinion—for their kindness and liberality of thought toward himself and the other officers of the court. He would have every opportunity to change his mind in the ensuing years when some of the same defense attorneys derailed his prosecution efforts in the 1877 Ellenton riot cases.[40]

As a Freedmen's Bureau officer, Stone had ample opportunity to observe the political struggles of the Reconstruction era. Too much of the "old rebel and proscriptive spirit" and "power of mob law" remained for Congress to allow local whites to control the state. Thus Congress enfranchised the former slaves, Stone believed, "as a political necessity" and not from "any special love of the blacks or a desire to make up for a long series of oppressions upon them or a belief in their fitness" for the responsibilities of citizenship. Like many other Northerners, however, Stone had concluded from the example of black Union soldiers that "the instincts of the race were right, and that only opportunity had been wanting for them to prove themselves worthy of the confidence of the country." Because many of the former slaves did not immediately understand the power and privilege that the United States had given them with the right to vote, it became the duty of the Freedmen's Bureau agents to educate them and help them through the initial stages of forming their political organizations. Stone enjoyed this "not . . . altogether disagreeable" new duty. He took pride not only in the important role he had played in organizing the local Republican party in South Carolina, but perhaps even more in the political aptitude of blacks whose loyalty to the Union and devotion to the Republican party demonstrated that "freedom was a blessing of which they were worthy."[41]

Many former Confederates, on the other hand, were still disfranchised in 1868, and most of the others refused to go to the polls with their former slaves. Hence they robbed themselves of any participation in the state constitutional convention, leaving the work to blacks, outsiders, and a few local white Republicans. When they awakened to the reality of the situation, whites began to seek black votes—not by recognizing blacks as equal participants in the political process but by appealing to the bonds between the races created during slavery. Astonished that whites considered the blacks so gullible, Stone dismissed their appeals to childhood playmates, family attachments, and "nursing from the same breast" as "mere twaddle."[42] Blacks understood clearly which party had freed them and which had sought to hold them in bondage. They would remain loyal to the party of Lincoln through the dark days of Reconstruction and well beyond—despite the violence they suffered as loyal members of the Republican Party.

William Stone thought he knew a better way for Southern whites to form political bonds with the freedmen. South Carolina whites could have won over the black voters, Stone believed, by truthfully admitting they did their best to hold them in bondage and had been whipped for their effort. Submission to the legal principles of Reconstruction and a sincere promise to make and enforce laws to protect black rights would have enabled white South Carolinians to lead the Reconstruction process. Had they done so, Reconstruction could have been very different. But such compromise was too great a strain for the "proud South Carolina aristocrat." While Stone's plan may well have been more peaceful, he acknowledged that "a thorough revolution in the body politic of the South" was probably necessary to create a real democracy in the South.[43]

Most Northerners assumed that the right to vote would empower blacks to take care of themselves. They naively expected that a rule of law sufficient to protect the former slaves in their rights as citizens would follow naturally from constitutional amendments and federal statutes. As Stone himself put it, "With the ballot in their hands, having a voice in choosing the officers of the state and of their district, and in making laws, it seems to me that they should not look longer to the General Government for assistance."[44] White South Carolinians had no intentions, however, of abiding by any law or constitutional amendment that made African Americans their political equals. Whatever the cost, they grimly determined to keep up the fight for political control of the state until the Republicans surrendered. Well after the end of Reconstruction, another "carpetbagger," Albion Tourgée, criticized the North for believing "that enfranchisement was all that was required to cure all the ills which hitherto had afflicted, or in the future might assail, the troublesome and pestiferous African." It was a "fool's errand," Tourgée wrote, to think that the North could "superimpose the civilization, the idea of the North, upon the South at a moment's notice."[45]

If Reconstruction was a "fool's errand," William Stone nevertheless gave it his best shot. William Stone's record ends abruptly with the completion of his service in the Freedmen's Bureau, but Stone continued his efforts on behalf of the freed people in South Carolina until 1877. He left the state in the fall of 1869, married Mary Taylor, the Quaker schoolteacher he had met in Aiken, then remained on active duty with the War Department in Washington, D.C., where he continued to "read law assiduously." He resigned from the army in August 1870, whereupon he and

Mary moved to Charleston. Admitted to practice by the South Carolina Supreme Court in December 1870, Stone joined the law firm of David T. Corbin, another white Northern Republican who had remained in South Carolina after serving in the Freedmen's Bureau. Corbin was a state senator, the attorney responsible for codifying South Carolina laws, and the United States district attorney for South Carolina, a position that kept him at odds with the majority of white South Carolinians. Corbin had married Mary's sister Carrie Taylor, another Pennsylvania Quaker who had come to South Carolina to teach the former slaves. The two families bought houses on adjoining lots in Charleston, where—despised by most white South Carolinians—they enjoyed being with family and the other Northerners who had settled in South Carolina. Corbin and Stone established a successful law partnership, and both remained active politically throughout the long period of Reconstruction. Stone was appointed assistant U.S. district attorney in 1871, a position he held until 1876. He also served as state attorney general for a short term during the governorship of Daniel H. Chamberlain, the last of the Northern Republican governors of South Carolina. When Corbin resigned as U.S. attorney, Stone took his place. Between them, the brothers-in-law represented the United States government in its most serious attempts to stop the violence and protect the voting rights of the state's black citizens: the Ku Klux Klan trials of 1871–72 and the Ellenton riot trials of 1877.[46] When President Rutherford Hayes removed the last of the federal troops from South Carolina in April 1877, the Stones recognized the futility of remaining in the state and moved to New York City. There Stone established another law firm, where he practiced until his death in 1897.

William Stone was an idealist and optimist who eventually had the idealism knocked out of him. As a Freedmen's Bureau agent and later as federal attorney and state attorney general, he promoted the rights of African Americans to equality under the law. But Stone had grossly underestimated the unyielding determination of white South Carolinians to preserve their time-honored tradition of white supremacy. When the federal government ceased to supply the muscle to keep the state's Republican Party in power, Stone realistically cut his losses and moved north. William Stone's Freedmen's Bureau report demonstrates his astute analysis of slavery's impact on every aspect of Southern life and his hope that constitutional change and free labor ideology could remake South Carolina into the image of New England. It was not to be. Nevertheless he had the satisfaction of knowing, as he stated in a letter to another Freedmen's Bureau agent, "We ourselves are not passive spectators of this great work; we have had a hand in the great struggle" to provide every American "his inalienable rights of liberty, and the pursuit of happiness."[47]

LOU FALKNER WILLIAMS

Notes

I would like to acknowledge the support of the Department of History at Kansas State University. Not only is it a congenial home institution, but it has funded the travel undertaken in conjuction with this research.

The epigraph is drawn from a letter in the Erastus W. Everson Collection, South Carolina Historical Society, Charleston, S.C.

1. William Stone has received little attention in historians' accounts of Reconstruction, possibly because his Freedmen's Bureau report, diaries, and other personal papers have remained in possession of his descendants. Nevertheless there are numerous interesting Stone documents in the following collections: David T. Corbin Papers, South Carolina Historical Society, Charleston, S.C.; Erastus W. Everson Collection, South Carolina Historical Society, Charleston, S.C.; Source Chronological Files of the Justice Department, RG 60, National Archives, Washington, D.C.; Freedmen's Bureau Records for South Carolina, National Archives, Washington, D.C.; and Martha Schofield Collection, Friends Library, Swarthmore College, Swarthmore, Pa. I have been fascinated with William Stone since I first encountered some of his letters in the Erastus W. Everson Collection while working on my dissertation. I am profoundly grateful to the Stone family for permission to use his private papers. I also want to thank W. Lewis Burke of the University of South Carolina Law School for his insightful comments on an earlier version of the introduction. Thanks, too, to my son Randy Williams for his editing skills and encouragement.

2. William Stone, *Bitter Freedom: William Stone's Record of Service in the Freedmen's Bureau* (Columbia: University of South Carolina Press, 2008). See pp. 5, 6, 101–2 for examples of Stone's sources.

3. Stone, *Bitter Freedom,* 101.

4. For an excellent introduction to the Freedmen's Bureau, see Randall M. Miller, "The Freedman's Bureau and Reconstruction: An Overview," in *The Freedmen's Bureau and Reconstruction: Reconsiderations*, ed. Paul A. Cimbala and Randall M. Miller (New York: Fordham University Press, 1999), xiii–xxxi.

5. Amos Bronson Alcott Web site, "Thomas Treadwell Stone, 1801–1895," http://alcott.net/alcott/home/champions/Stone.html (accessed March 22, 2008); quotation from Thomas T. Stone, *The Martyr of Freedom: A Discourse Delivered at East Machias, November 30, and at Machias, December 7, 1837* (Boston: Isaac Knapp,

1838), 20–21, 26. For biographical information on Thomas Treadwell Stone, see Samuel Atkins Eliot, *Heralds of a Liberal Faith,* vol. 3, *The Preachers* (Boston: American Unitarian Association, 1910), 358–62.

6. William Stone to Martha Schofield, May 11, 1869, Martha Schofield Collection, Friends Library, Swarthmore College, Swarthmore, Pa.

7. William Stone, boyhood diary, passim, Stone Family Archives; quote from May 9, 1858.

8. Stone, boyhood diary, passim; *Bitter Freedom*, 5.

9. Stone, boyhood diary, September 5–November 6, 1860.

10. William Stone to My Dear Father [Thomas Stone], November 21, 1860, Stone Family Archives.

11. See Steven A. Channing, *Crisis of Fear: Secession in South Carolina* (New York: Norton, 1970).

12. William Stone, Civil War diary, passim, Stone Family Archives.

13. Ibid., June 25, 1862; *Civil War Almanac*, June 25, 1862 (New York: World Almanac Publications, 1983), 104.

14. Stone, Civil War diary, April 12, 1863; Massachusetts Civil War Research Center, "Nineteenth Regiment Massachusetts Volunteer Infantry," http://www.Massachusettscivilwar.com/histories.asp (accessed April 24, 2007).

15. Stone, Civil War diary.

16. Ibid., July 2, 3, and 5, 1863; "Nineteenth Regiment."

17. Stone, *Bitter Freedom,* 67.

18. Eric Foner, *Free Soil, Free Labor, Free Men: The Ideology of the Republican Party before the Civil War* (New York: Oxford, 1970), 40–72.

19. Gavin Wright, *Old South, New South: Revolutions in the Southern Economy since the Civil War* (1986; repr., Baton Rouge: Louisiana State University Press, 1996), 17–31. Unlike cotton, rice cultivation depended on the tidal flows in the Sea Islands and coastal areas to flood and drain the fields. Hence rice planters, unlike cotton planters, did not have the option of moving west when their fields were exhausted.

20. On the genesis of the Republican Party, see Foner, *Free Soil, Free Labor, Free Men.*

21. Stone, *Bitter Freedom,* 6, 18.

22. Ibid., 6, 17–18.

23. Ibid., 21; Stone's boyhood diary records his frequent attendance at temperance meetings; the Civil War diary, however, demonstrates that he was not a teetotaler.

24. Ibid., 22, 18–19. Note that Stone's analysis of the slave economy dovetails closely with economic historian Gavin Wright's explanation above. Stone seems to lump white South Carolinians into two groups: planters and poor whites. It is important to note that the majority of white South Carolinians did not own slaves. Planters (those with twenty or more slaves) were a very small percentage of the

population. Yeoman farmers and small slaveholders worked hard to make their living from the soil.

25. Ibid., 19; Deborah Gray White, "Female Slaves in the Plantation South," in *Before Freedom Came: African-American Life in the Antebellum South*, ed. Edward D. C. Campbell Jr. with Kym S. Rice (Richmond: University Press of Virginia, 1991), 104–5; Kenneth M. Stampp, *The Peculiar Institution: Slavery in the Ante-Bellum South* (New York: Vintage, 1964), 245–51.

26. Stone, *Bitter Freedom,* 20–22. Curiously, Stone does not discuss the sexual exploitation of black women by white men, which was a central theme of abolitionist protest throughout the antebellum years.

27. Ibid., 20–22.

28. Martin Abbott, *The Freedmen's Bureau in South Carolina, 1865*–1872 (Chapel Hill: University of North Carolina, 1967), 131–32. For Stone's account of the records he was required to keep, see Stone, *Bitter Freedom,* 35.

29. On political violence and the federal government's efforts to prosecute see Lou Falkner Williams, *The Great South Carolina Ku Klux Klan Trials, 1871–1872* (Athens: University of Georgia Press, 1996).

30. Abbott, *Freedmen's Bureau,* 37–44.

31. LaWanda Cox, "General O. O. Howard and the 'Misrepresented Bureau,'" in *Freedom, Racism, and Reconstruction: Collected Writings of LaWanda Cox*, ed. Donald G. Nieman (Athens: University of Georgia Press, 1997), 166–68.

32. Stone, *Bitter Freedom,* 48–51

33. See, for example, William S. McFeely, *Yankee Stepfather: General O. O. Howard and the Freedmen* (New York: Norton, 1994); Cox, "Misrepresented Bureau," 149–52, quote from p. 151.

34. Stone, *Bitter Freedom,* 8–9. Orville Vernon Burton, *In My Father's House Are Many Mansions: Family and Community in Edgefield, South* Carolina (Chapel Hill: University of North Carolina Press, 1985), 268–69. On contract labor system, see Donald G. Nieman, *To Set the Law in Motion: The Freedmen's Bureau and the Legal Rights of Blacks, 1865–1868* (Millwood, N.Y.: KTO, 1979), 35–66.

35. Stone, *Bitter Freedom,* 35–39.

36. Katherine Smedley, *Martha Schofield and the Re-education of the South, 1839–1916* (Lewiston, N.Y.: Edward Mellen, 1987), 104–6.

37. Stone, *Bitter Freedom,* 14–15.

38. Ibid., 39.

39. Ibid., 41–45. Sessions of the provost court were also held at Barnwell and Aiken, which was still a part of Edgefield County. Stone's bureau district included both Edgefield and Barnwell counties.

40. Ibid., 4, 45. On Stone's efforts as federal prosecutor, see Lou Falkner Williams, "Federal Enforcement in the Post-Redemption South: The Ellenton Riot Case," in *Local Matters: Race, Crime, and Justice in the Nineteenth-Century South*,

ed. Christopher Waldrep and Donald G. Nieman (Athens: University of Georgia Press, 2001), 172–99.

41. Stone, *Bitter Freedom,* 56–60.

42. Ibid., 59–60.

43. Ibid., 61.

44. Ibid., 101.

45. Albion W. Tourgée, *A Fool's Errand: A Novel of the South during Reconstruction* (1879; repr., Prospect Heights, Ill.: Waveland Press, 1991), 251, 380–81.

46. On the Klan trials, see Williams, *Ku Klux Klan Trials.* See also Williams, "Federal Enforcement of Black Rights."

47. William Stone to Erastus Everson, December 20, 1867, Erastus W. Everson Collection, South Carolina Historical Society, Charleston, S.C.

A Record of Service in the Freedmen's Bureau

By 1 Lieut. William Stone, 45th Inf., U.S.A.

[Part I]

IT WAS ON THE 16TH DAY of Jan. 1866, that I first received orders from the Adjutant General's Office, Washington to report by letter to General [Oliver O.] Howard, Commissioner of the Freedmen's Bureau for assignment to duty.

I was then on duty at the Office of the Acting Assistant Provost Marshal General and Chief Mustering Officer, Philadelphia, holding the rank of Captain, Seventh Regiment Veteran Reserve Corps, and Brevet Major of Volunteers.

I was detained as a witness before the United States District Court until the latter part of February, and on the 2nd of March, 1866 I received orders to report to Brig. Gen. R[obert] K. Scott, Assistant Commissioner for the State of South Carolina at Charleston, for assignment.

A few days after, I left for Charleston, arriving there March 12.

I chose the route via Richmond and Wilmington, N.C., wishing to pass through Fredericksburg and the battlefields around Petersburg as well as to see Richmond, before which in 1862 we encamped, and the country between Washington and Charleston.

The railroads were in very bad condition and very few passengers were carried. After leaving Richmond, I think the trains consisted of but one passenger and the usual baggage cars.

While waiting in Manchester, opposite Richmond, on a dark, cold March morning for the train, I had occasion to assist a young lady whom I took to be a "Yankee school-marm" about her baggage, and afterwards found her to be a Miss Sproat of Taunton, Mass. going to Wilmington, N.C. to teach a colored school under the auspices of Bishop [Thomas] Atkinson of the Episcopal Church in N.C.

Both of us being Massachusetts Yankees, we naturally preferred each others society to that of the southerners on the train.

As the bridges across the Roanoke River had been destroyed, the train ran up to Gaston, and at that point passengers and baggage were ferried across in flat bottom boats in primitive style.

From Petersburg south, the country was one monotonous level covered with the heavy pine woods for which North Carolina is noted. Occasionally we would pass through some dirty settlement of unpainted weather-stained houses dignified by the name of a town, and sometimes we would pass large clearings where the negroes were preparing to plant the season's crops.

Everything looked old, rickety and miserable, and furnished a striking contrast to the well-tilled, neat and thrifty farms of Pennsylvania, New Jersey, and New England.

Here and there appeared a turpentine still with its quota of homely, rough barrels filled with rosin awaiting buyers or transportation.

We reached Wilmington early in the morning and then I left my companion to the new scenes and trials which were inevitable to such a position as hers.

As we crossed the Cape Fear River on an old steam ferry boat, the sun was just rising and the grass and trees were covered with a heavy frost. The chilly air was more cutting than our cold winter winds, and the teeth of all the passengers chattered like monkeys.

On the boat, I met Mr. Galvin of Philadelphia and Mr. Kelly of Calais, Maine who were going to Jacksonville, Fla. They remained in Charleston a few days, and we went about a good deal together there.

From Wilmington, we went to Florence reaching there about six o'clock P.M. The appearance of the country was much the same as that of North Carolina.

It was cold when we reached Florence, and the fire of pitch pine which was built for our comfort in the sitting room of the hotel was very comfortable.

Here we had only half a night's sleep having to get up at one and a half o'clock to take cars for Charleston. We had to cross the Santee River in flat boats, an operation which delayed us about an hour.

Reached Charleston and remained there until the 17th, just a week.

While in Charleston, made the acquaintance of Mr. E. G. Browne of Newbern, but a native of Essex Co. Mass. who had formerly done business in Charleston. With him I went a good deal about the city and also down to Mt. Pleasant, taking a pleasant sail over there one afternoon.[1]

The appearance of Charleston plainly showed how much it had felt the effects of the war. The lower part of the city towards the Battery was unpaved and the dust was terrible. On the Battery was the old Rebel earthwork on which were mounted the Armstrong guns which had been sent from England.

One had burst at the first discharge and shattered terribly many of the fine houses opposite it.

The view down the harbor from the Battery was very fine and over the ruins of Sumter it was pleasant to see the Stars and Stripes waving. A Revenue cutter and one or two gun boats were lying off the city and quite a number of vessels were in the harbor.

At a street corner near one of the wharves was pointed out the old whipping post to which negroes and criminals used to be tied to be flogged, but its further use had been forbidden by General Sickles, the Department Commander.

Over the "burnt district" the grass had already grown, and goats wandered about the ruins making the most of their opportunities.

The fire which destroyed this portion of the city originated in December 1861 from a carpenter's shop on East Bay St., I think, and swept almost across the peninsula carrying everything before it. It was a sad prospect when I was there, and I do not think it has been rebuilt.

Many of the houses in Charleston had roofs of brick tiles unlike anything I had ever seen before. In some instances these had been crushed by some shell from our fleet or from the "Swamp Angel" on Morris Island.[2]

Other houses were discolored by a greenish moss which gave them a very ancient appearance.

An Opera Troupe arrived at Charleston when I was there and I went one evening with Mr. Galvin to hear "Il Trovatore." The troupe was small, the stage arrangements defective, and the Hall unsuited to such performances, but nevertheless there was quite a large audience of the "wealth and beauty," as the papers said, of Charleston. During the evening, Gen'l [Daniel E.] Sickles and some of his staff came in, in uniform and it was very gratifying to see with what complacency he bore the looks of hatred and scorn with which many regarded him. He represented the power of the United States and in that rebellious city any sort of display of it was agreeable to me.

But it is not my intent to describe Charleston. Other officers who have been stationed there longer know the history of its vicissitudes better than I, and my recollections of it may be imperfect.

With one thing I was most forcibly struck, and that was the entire lack of enterprise on the part of the citizens and the look of hopeless indifference which the old residents wore. Trade seemed dull, drays moved lazily along the street, negroes congregated in the front of Bureau Headquarters for rations, and even the auctioneers did not seem to invite sales with ordinary animation.

As I have not been there since 1866, I do not know whether it has undergone much change in these respects.

On the 14th of March received orders to go to Anderson to establish an office, and on the following day concluded my preparations for the purpose, called on Gen'l Scott, hunted in vain for a Digest of the Laws of So. Ca., and finally contented myself with the purchase of Blackstone's Commentaries, a lucky purchase, and one that has proved of inestimable value.

On the 16th of March I left Charleston for my new station having to go to Hamburg first,[3] however, to report to Col. [Arthur F.] Devereaux, an old Philadelphia acquaintance and then Acting Assistant Commissioner.

Left Charleston at 6 A.M. and reached Hamburg the next morning about 4 o'clock. From Branchville to Aiken the railroad had been completely destroyed by Sherman and it had been rebuilt only as far as Williston.

Along the road were the evidences of Sherman's march. Rail fences were destroyed. Half burned sleepers and bent rails were everywhere in sight and piles of ashes indicated where the bivouacs had been. Unsightly chimneys not yet overgrown with foliage showed the sadder features of war. Some ingenious parties had, in the villages, set fires under the trees and twisted into knots or coils the heated rails making their further use impossible. In Williston I saw several of such coils. Several times since I have passed over the same route but each time the traces of war were less visible until now hardly a remark is made on the subject.

From Williston to Johnson's [Turn Out, now Montmorenci] a distance of sixteen miles, we had to go by stage. To do this six hours were necessary over a heavy, bad road, with nothing to interest one.

By reference to a journal I kept at that time, I find that the other passengers in the old ambulance in which I rode were Southerners who spent most of their time in abusing Massachusetts and the Freedmen's Bureau. The driver was the most agreeable person, who had served in the rebel army in the 61st Georgia Reg't and who told me that of six of his brothers who served during the war, five had been killed. I do not know who this man was.

The road from Williston to Johnson's I know very well now but at that time I had little expectation or desire to see it again. At Johnson's we got something to eat, but at what house I have never yet found out. We left there about midnight in some miserable cars, which are now about Aiken and were four hours in getting to Hamburg, a distance of twenty-two miles.

On the train was a very large fat man whose conversation indicated that he was a minister but whose appearance was decidedly unclerical. He talked loud and was a fierce secessionist. After coming to Aiken on duty, I met him several times and found his name was Pickett and that he was a Methodist preacher at Graniteville. He is a very worthy, kind man, formerly a slave-holder, and very well educated. His political opinions are not such as I fancy, still for the man personally I have great respect. He called to see me last spring (1868) to get aid for a colored school in Graniteville.

As I was fresh from the North and unaccustomed to all Southern towns, I was much surprised on reaching Hamburg to find a nailed up railroad station and no signs of life anywhere. But my baggage was out and I could not leave it to seek a hotel so I sat on my trunk and wrapped my overcoat about me to keep off the chilly cold which came up from the Savannah. It was dark and I did not know where to look for the town, and for two hours I waited with such patience as I could for daylight. When it came, my surprise was great to find that instead of a large, thriving town of three or four thousand inhabitants, I had got into a struggling, decaying village all ready to be washed away by the first freshet in the Savannah. I have since learned that something [*sic*; nothing] more than a "local habitation and a name" on a map is necessary to constitute a Southern town.

However I at last found a hotel into which one had to step downwards from the side-walk, and the front entry and stairs of which were sleeping places for goats, and in due time had a room and breakfast.

I found here Lieut. [George P.] McDougall who treated me very kindly although no comforts had the place afforded him. During the forenoon Col. Devereaux came over from Augusta to his office, and with him had quite a pleasant chat. During the day I went over to Augusta which seemed quite like a large Southern town. It escaped the ravages of war, and seemed really an enterprising place. Here Col. Devereaux lived in preference to his uncomfortable office in Hamburg.

I had intended to leave Hamburg the following night but as the train did not stop, had to remain over another day. But I found Rev. Henry Edes in Augusta and as the day was Sunday, passed most of it with him very pleasantly going to the white Baptist church in the morning and to a colored church in the afternoon.

Mr. Edes had been sent down as a missionary by the American Unitarian Association, but he found it impossible to get hearers at his religious services. He was a Yankee and a Unitarian which were quite enough to keep the Southern people away, and then there were no others scarcely in Augusta. The knowledge of either fact would have prevented his meeting any success but the double disadvantage virtually made his enterprise a failure.

Monday night, March 19th I left Hamburg and went back to Branchville by the same means that I had gone to Hamburg. We left Johnson's at midnight and reached Williston at six o'clock where we got breakfast.

The journey from Branchville to Columbia was made in four hours and one half. The road was in better condition than the Augusta branch but the appearance of the country was not pleasant. Everything was unsettled, the people (whites) were disheartened and it seemed almost like a foreign country. A few weeks since, when passing over this road, the fields were in many places white with cotton or covered with good crops of corn. Still, thousands of acres of good land are lying idle waiting for someone to cultivate and improve them.

In my Journal I wrote that "Columbia was a most beautiful city at one time but the ruins of the fire still show the awful destruction caused by the war." The same can be written of that city today. Broad streets well shaded by deciduous trees, handsome gardens filled with rare plants, large comfortable houses indicating taste and wealth have yet preserved the beauty of the place. But the tall chimneys blackened with smoke and cracked with heat—[General William T.] Sherman's Sentinels the people call them—the broken walls, the yards turned into vegetable gardens, the cellars, half filled with broken bricks and rubbish, still show how terribly the people must have suffered for their share in the rebellion.

It is needless to say that it is almost a cardinal doctrine of the Southern creed that Sherman ordered the destruction of this place. Neither his own reports nor those of his subordinate officers can convince a Southerner of the contrary. My friend, Mr. Edwin James of Philadelphia, had in 1865 an autographed letter from Gen'l Sherman reiterating the truth of his official reports.

Of course, no one who knows anything about a large army in time of war would undertake to deny that individual soldiers could and very likely would commit with impunity many acts which would throw disgrace upon a whole command. In a large city like Columbia where men must have been scattered, and where unusual opportunities for pillage were presented, it is more than probable that many of them set fire to houses which might otherwise have escaped.[4]

I have in my own experience seen instances of pillage which were entirely the work of individuals acting in defiance of standing orders.

At Charles City C.H., Va. on the march from Harrison's Landing to Williamsburg in August, 1862, the buildings were broken open by our troops and the public records scattered to the winds. No one at the time regarded it as a serious matter and for my own part I was much pleased with some old records I picked up but which I subsequently lost at Antietam—dating back to the reign of George Third. It is only after the war closed and we had the opportunity of reflecting upon such acts that we realized their wantonness. It would, however, be manifestly unjust to make the Government or the Commanding General responsible for such deeds.

Columbia has been rebuilt in part but it will be many years before it can be as it was before the war.

From Columbia I went by rail and stage to Anderson. The road had been washed nearly away by a freshet of the Broad River and about nine miles of the way had to be made in stages. After leaving Allston, the country became more rolling and the farms better. Still they had an un-thrifty look not pleasant to Northern eyes.

On the train was a Southern lady who had a transportation order from the government. She was dressed in black and appeared quite poor. By her conversation with others, however, I found that she was an ardent secessionist and down on the "Yankees." Nevertheless she was willing to accept favors of the very Government she would gladly have seen destroyed.

It was not long before I found that very few persons hesitated to receive any sort of assistance from Bureau officers or Military Commanders no matter how much they might dislike them. In fact, I was of the opinion that it was regarded as a creditable and smart thing to get anything out of the Government, and that opinion I have had no occasion to change.

After a long tedious ride I arrived at Anderson about nine o'clock P.M. on the 21st of March. An Army wagon which happened to be at the station took me and my baggage to the hotel a third of a mile distant where I found accommodations.

The next day I obtained an office in a building occupied by Col. [John Marshall] Brown of the 1st Battalion Maine Volunteers and issued a circular assuming charge of Freedmen's affairs for Anderson District. Here then, I entered upon a new phase of Army experience.

Office Duty at Anderson

Immediately upon assuming charge of Freedmen's affairs, I went to work upon my new duties.

I had obtained at Charleston a file of General Orders and circulars governing the Bureau, and on my way to Anderson had found time to read them carefully and consider of their bearing. Such attention as the Freedmen had received was from some officers temporarily detailed for the purpose, and a board for approving contracts composed of an officer and two civilians. The civilians were paid by a tax on each contract approved.

As I could find no instructions to collect such a tax and no provision for paying civilians for such duty, I took the entire responsibility for approving or disapproving upon myself and received from the Board a large pile of contracts written upon papers of every size and color and with such skill in chirography—with some exceptions—as a Northern schoolboy not yet in his teens usually exhibits. Some of these were approved and some were not, some were stamped and others were unstamped; a few were on printed forms but the greater number were written.

From the Commanding Officer of the troops, I obtained an enlisted man to help compare the two copies of each contract with the original and to endorse them. In the course of a few weeks all had been through with and were numbered and arranged and filed away alphabetically.

The terms usually paid hands were one third of the crop, the laborer paying for his own food and clothing, or one fourth of the crop with the employer feeding the laborer, or six or seven dollars a month and "patches" for a garden of potatoes or rice.

Some paid the merest pittance and their contracts were, of course, disapproved. One or two, as if in defiance of the new order of things, agreed to feed and clothe and treat their laborers just as they had done while they were slaves. Before the summer, however, most of these men were convinced of the necessity of paying good wages to their hands.

The original contract after approval was filed in the office, and a copy was given to the employer and a copy to the freedmen.

While approving contracts, complaints would be made from time to time of their violation by one party or the other, generally by the employer, and a letter would be written or a man sent to show the one complained of the necessity of their observance of their obligation. It was seldom that more than one complaint would be made by the same person.

I was relieved from duty at Anderson in September by Lieut. McDougall who reported at the end of the year that everything went on well there.

Where everything was new and a great deal was left to the judgement of officers, of course questions of all sorts would be presented for decision and it required much thought often to know how to dispose of them. Any decision, almost, was better than none, and the nearer one could arrive at a sensible conclusion—even though not strictly legal—the better it would be for all parties.

The most difficult questions were those arising from the marriage relation, and indeed throughout my whole experience, I have found this to be the case. The orders of the Bureau were too general to meet the various conditions of the freed people, and the State laws were in abeyance while the State was under martial law. It can easily be seen that great care was necessary in determining how far the mutual rights and privileges of husband and wife extended.

One of the first instances of this sort I had to deal with was the case of a wife who had become angry with her husband who was living at Belton, twelve miles distant, and refused to live with him. After many vehement declarations that she would die first, etc., by a rather arbitrary stretch of authority, I told her she must go back to him and dismissed her. I soon after learned that she did go back and was living very quietly and pleasantly with him.

In approving contracts, hearing and investigating complaints, and in one or two instances exercising judicial functions, making reports and conducting necessary correspondence, I passed my time in the office, devoting any spare moments I could to the reading of [*Commentaries on the Laws of England* by William] Blackstone into which, until then, I had never looked, and Pressley's "Law of Magistrates" [Benjamin C. Pressley's *The Law of Magistrates and Constables in the State of South-Carolina*].[5] Before the summer was over, the hardest part of the work was done and I had some leisure to ride horseback, read, etc.

I had forgotten to class among my duties the issue of rations to destitute freed people once a week or thereabouts. The actual issue was made by the Post Commissary on orders which were given to the applicants signed by me. On the days for issuing rations we saw a pitiable set of poor creatures who had worn out the best of the years of their lives in the service of others without thanks or reward, having been left by them utterly destitute to seek their food where they could.

I know they justified themselves under the plea that slaves were their only property and by emancipating them they were deprived of the means of assisting them, and probably others in their situation would have said and done the same. Still it seemed hard that the poor old people, almost helpless by reason of age and hard work, should receive no assistance from those who had been enriched by their labor in earlier years.

Among these old people was a helpless old man who was said to be over one hundred years old, who used to sit in the sun or crouch over a smouldering fire even in the hottest days of summer. He was a native African, and was brought to this country before the slave trade had been made piratical.[6] He could barely crawl about the yard, and it was almost impossible to understand his speech.

From twenty to thirty of these people were kept from starvation by the bureau until August 1866 when the issue of rations was discontinued.

Military Forces at Anderson

The officers of the bureau were so much dependent on the military forces for assistance in carrying out their orders any account which would make no reference to them would be incomplete.

On going to Anderson, I found that it was the headquarters of a Military Sub District embracing Anderson, Pickens, Abbeville, and, I think, Greenville districts. Lt. Col. Brown of the First Battalion Maine Volunteer

Infantry was in command and the detachments of his Battalion were stationed at the Court House towns in Anderson, Abbeville, Greenville, and at Walhalla in Pickens.

His troops were chiefly from Eastern Maine and were generally raw young soldiers. They were soon relieved and were sent home to be mustered out. Col. Brown was from Eastport, and was a lawyer by profession. He was, I think, a graduate of Brown University. He was not a popular officer among the citizens and not a good disciplinarian, but I found him an agreeable companion and was indebted to him for many valuable suggestions about the course to be pursued by an officer in dealing with the citizens and obtained from him much information.

When I first went to Anderson, the people were greatly interested and somewhat excited at the trial which was then progressing in Charleston before a Military Commission of three or four citizens for the murder of three of Col. Brown's soldiers at Brown's Ferry on the Savannah River a few months before.

The soldiers were guarding a quantity of cotton seized by the government which was claimed by a man named [Crawford] Keyes living about two miles from the Court House. They were found afterwards in the river, shot through the head.

Keyes was arrested, together with two others named Bryan and Stowes, and were the ones on trial at Charleston. I never read the proceedings of the trial although they were published in full in the newspapers from day to day. The people generally believed them to be innocent, particularly Keyes who was wealthy and was called respectable. However they were found guilty by the Commission and were sentenced to be hanged, which sentence was confirmed by Gen. Sickles. The proceedings, as in all such cases, had to be sent to the President for final action. He did not disapprove the proceedings, finding or sentence, but commuted the sentence to imprisonment for life, or for a term of years, I forget which, at the Dry Tortugas whither they were sent.

During the summer, however, they were removed to Fort Delaware, brought before a United States Court on a writ of Habeas Corpus, and released on the ground of the illegality of the Commission. They returned to Anderson after I had left there and were received—as I learned from the officers on duty there—with open arms.

Before I went to Anderson, many outrages upon soldiers and negroes had been committed by a band of desperadoes among whom were Mansus

[Manson S. "Mance"] Jolly, Tom Sargent, Pete Keyes, Brown and others. They always evaded arrest, and were no doubt countenanced and encouraged by many of the citizens. In the various changes which were occurring in the military commanders at that time and the imperfect records which were kept, no authentic account was had of the acts of these men. They were a terror to the free people and a curse to the District. Gov. [James L.] Orr did all he could to secure their arrest but without success.

Col. Brown sent many parties after these men but never arrested one, nor has one of them been arrested yet that I have heard of.

Col. Brown was relieved by a Lieut. [Livensbarger?] of an Illinois Regiment or an Ohio Regiment. I do not remember which. He was an inefficient, careless officer and accomplished nothing. His command was soon mustered out of service and his place was taken by Lt. Col. [Benjamin Bixby] Murray of the 15th Maine Volunteers with two or three companies. This was a veteran regiment and officers and men had seen service in Louisiana and the Shenandoah Valley, but were anxious to get home. Col. Murray cooperated with me as far as was necessary, and our relations to each other were pleasant.

During the summer this regiment was mustered out and Co. "I" of the 8th Infantry in command of Lieut. (now Capt.) [Charles?] Snyder relieved that portion on duty at Anderson. Lieut. Snyder was an old Philadelphia acquaintance, and with him my relations were very agreeable. So too were they with Col. [Gilman D.] Smith who was Captain of the Company and who soon relieved Lieut. Snyder. Some of his officers I liked very much, particularly the Surgeon, Dr. Higgins whose wife was there with him. With him, I have, by means of a correspondence, kept up an acquaintance which is very pleasant.

Col. Smith had his wife with him, and hers was the only congenial lady's society the officers had.

To all the officers whose acquaintance I made at Anderson am I indebted for many courtesies and much pleasant intercourse. They did much to relieve what otherwise would have been a most disagreeable life.

Schools

Immediately upon going to Anderson I made efforts to have a Freedmen's School established at the Court House. The leading freedmen were anxious to have one, and the citizens made no opposition. The Town Council agreed to allow the use of an unoccupied brick school house for the purpose, and Col. Brown detailed one of his private soldiers who was a Methodist minister as teacher. He was assisted by a colored man of some intelligence, and soon quite a large school was in operation.

But this teacher could not be kept long, and I was very glad when Gov. Orr and Mr. Crayton called on me and recommended one of their citizens, a Mr. Crawford, as teacher. After some talk with Mr. Crawford, he consented to teach if he could secure an appointment. After a while I learned that the Freedmen's Union Commission would employ him. He at once went to work earnestly and continued to teach steadily until last July (1867). His school generally numbered over one hundred scholars.

One of the leading colored men at Anderson who took much pains in starting and sustaining the school was a blacksmith named Kennedy. He had been a slave of Judge [Joseph N.] Whitner, a prominent citizen, and was a Baptist preacher. I always found him an honest hard-working man, and he frequently called to see me about the interests of the freed people. In August of 1868 he was attending a "protracted" meeting in Ruckersville, Ga. when he received warnings to leave. He did so but on his way home he was enticed from his buggy, dragged into the bushes, and murdered. A young boy, his grandson, was with him at the time but could not identify the murderers. These facts I learned from Z. Taylor, Esq. of Anderson C.H.

When this school was first started, the teacher found written in chalk on the door, "Take Notice. Let the first one who opens this door look out for himself for I will blow his brains out, McCreery." "Nigger School." It is hardly necessary to say that this sanguinary threat was never carried into execution.

After the school at Anderson C.H. was fairly under way, Sunday schools began to be started in different portions of the district. The Presbyterian Society also took a great interest in teaching the blacks at a Sunday school organized for them, and every Sunday afternoon which could be devoted to it their church was filled with the colored people of all ages and denominations. With the Pastor of the Society, Rev. William Stratton, I was on excellent terms and I am glad to bear testimony to the untiring energy and zeal which he showed in his efforts to improve the freedmen.

Mr. Norris, a parishioner of his who lived about four miles from the village, had a colored school on his own place which he and his children taught. While I was in Anderson, the other denominations made no efforts to teach colored people in their Sunday schools.

The success of the Anderson school being assured, the colored people of Belton applied for a school. They had received a lot of land and an old church as a gift and found that an old white teacher, Mr. P. L. Walker, would undertake the conduct of the school. But as the colored people could not undertake to pay him a salary and nothing could be obtained through the Superintendent of Education, I wrote to friends in Salem and to my brother Alfred in Providence to enlist their sympathies. In this way I succeeded in getting enough to keep the school going for a few months until the Salem, Mass. Freedmen's Aid Society adopted him as a teacher. They have continued to employ him ever since with the exception of one or two months.

Mr. Walker, at the beginning of the war, was suspected of entertaining Union sentiments and as I learned from good authority was cited to appear before a self-constituted vigilance committee at Belton to answer to that charge. The judge was, I think, a Baptist minister named Martin and the jury was composed of the necessary numbers of "sound" white citizens.

The accused, not wishing to trust himself to the tender mercies of such a tribunal, did not appear so the trial went on without him. He was found guilty and received some sentence, but as he kept out of sight for some time, he did not undergo it.

When he first started the school some threats were made against him which caused him to give it up for a few days but, on assuring him of military protection if necessary, he went on and to this time has been in no way interfered with.

It is satisfactory to record that both Mr. Crawford and Mr. Walker, although Southern men and to a certain extent sharing in the prejudices against the colored people, soon became interested in their work and satisfied of the capacity of the colored children to acquire knowledge.

The citizens, too, in Anderson and Belton soon took a sort of interest in the schools and were glad to see them going on.

At Pendleton, Williamston, and one or two other points, good schools could have been established if money could have been obtained to pay the teachers. For this purpose the Government appropriated nothing. The freed people themselves or the Freedmen's Aid Societies of the North paid for the services of every teacher among the freedmen.

It would be impossible to estimate the amount of good which has been accomplished through these Aid Societies. To say nothing of the immediate results of teaching the freed children the rudiments of knowledge. The prejudice against colored schools was attacked and often overthrown, the interest of the parents was excited in the welfare of their children, their self-respect increased and a new field of improvement was opened to them. No missionary enterprise of this generation has promised or accomplished so great results as this movement for raising up and educating the emancipated blacks of the South.

Nothing given for this cause has been thrown away. It would, of course, be unreasonable to look for any remarkable change in the general condition of the freed people of this generation in consequence of these schools. Where so much ignorance has existed, where so little attention has been paid to the proper training of the blacks, where churches have upheld the divinity of the Institution of Slavery and have even held slaves as property, where at a time of fancied necessity no regard has been paid to the holiest and most sacred ties of marriage and kindred, the sensibilities of these oppressed people must have been blunted and their moral natures perverted. Time and experience, with much patient labor and great charity can alone raise them to the full dignity of manhood and womanhood.

Government

All the time when I was in Anderson District, the military authorities were regarded as superior to the civil. In 1865 the Legislature of the State had met and passed a set of laws which denied to the freedmen the same rights which belonged to the whites.[7] They were not allowed to give evidence before the courts on the same footing with whites, offences committed by them were punished differently from those committed by whites, and a new court was established providing for their trial in capital cases without an indictment by a Grand Jury. A code of laws very elaborate and in some respects unobjectionable was adopted for their government, but as it recognized an unwarranted distinction in the privileges of the two classes it was never enforced. In every respect they were hampered and restricted in their rights.

On the first of January, 1866, General Sickles, then in command of the Department of South Carolina, published General Order No. 1, providing that all laws should be alike applicable to all inhabitants. It also provided that the right of all loyal and well-disposed inhabitants to bear arms should not be infringed, that corporal punishment should not be inflicted, and that all injuries to person or property, committed by or upon freed persons should be punished in the manner provided by the laws of So. Carolina for like injuries to the persons or property of citizens thereof.

Provost Courts were established to try crimes committed by and upon freedmen and controversies between freedmen and whites, and to this tribunal I referred such cases as I could not myself settle. During my stay in Anderson I referred very few cases to it. Small cases I usually succeeded in settling without difficulty, and in graver ones the parties accused generally evaded arrest.

Congress having passed the "Civil Rights" bill April 9, 1866, it became necessary for the State to modify its laws to conform to its provisions. For this purpose Gov. Orr called a special session of the General Assembly in the summer of 1866 which passed a Bill doing away with all legal discriminations against the colored people except so far as to prohibit their intermarriage with whites. At the same session, a law was passed allowing all persons to testify before the courts without regard to their interest in a case, leaving to the jury to decide upon the weight of the testimony.

By this legislation, the jurisdiction of the civil authorities was virtually extended to all cases except those against officers and soldiers of the United States, although it was not until the first of October that General Sickles directed a transfer of cases before military tribunals to the civil courts.

In such a mixture of military and civil rule there were, of course, many disadvantages. The members of Provost Courts were often men without legal knowledge or experience, not familiar with the rules of evidence, and unaccustomed to weighing testimony. Still they had generally a correct notion of substantial justice and probably rendered fair decisions, if not strictly legal ones. It would have been unsafe to allow the ordinary courts, composed of men who had opposed the General Government and the Emancipation of the slaves and who looked upon the freed people as not entitled to the benefit of such laws as affected the whites, to try cases in which they were concerned.

The testimony of blacks against whites would not have been taken, and many a criminal would have escaped his proper punishment. Before Provost Courts, the law was administered impartially, and punishment was generally sure to follow crime.

As the jurisdiction of Provost Courts was limited to minor offences, they could not impose fines exceeding one hundred dollars or imprison for a period longer than two months.

Felonies were tried before Military Commissions composed of army officers, the proceedings of which were recorded with as much precision as those of Court Martials, and every sentence had to be confirmed by the Commanding General.

A term of the Civil Court (Common Pleas and General Sessions) was held just before I went to Anderson but no civil court was held while I was there. The next regular term would have been in September or October.

District Courts had been established to meet once in two months but, owing to the causes stated above, they did not meet until after I was relieved.

One must regret any interruption in the ordinary course of the civil law, but the Rebellion so changed the condition of things in the South, military rule became necessarily superior to the civil, and to its operation was due in a great measure the protection of all classes of citizens.

Resources

The resources of Anderson were but partially developed owing to the smallness of the population compared with its extent of territory and the blighting influence of slave labor.

The surface was rolling and generally susceptible of cultivation. I am not able to describe its geological formation but the soil was generally red clay except in the river bottoms, much resembling that in Pennsylvania and New Jersey near the Alleghanies.

Numerous streams flow through it, the principal ones being the Seneca and Rocky Rivers. The Savannah formed its southwestern and the Saluda its northeastern boundary. Its water power is sufficient to carry hundreds of mills but only one or two are there besides the usual small grist and saw mills.

The woods contain oak, hickory, chestnut, and pine, and could furnish thousands of feet of lumber.

The uplands can produce excellent cotton and tobacco, and the bottom lands produce fine crops of corn. In the swamps, rice will mature nearly every year, and the smaller cereals, garden vegetables, sweet potatoes, etc. will grow anywhere. The fig is abundant; apples, pears, peaches, plums and the smaller fruits can be easily raised, and old fields furnish good pasturage nearly all the year.

At Anderson, C.H., the climate is very healthy. The summers are not as hot although longer than ours in New England, and the winter is short.

Sudden changes, however, are frequent and snow fell there on the 26th of March.

Gov. Orr, in the course of a conversation, told me he regarded that district as one of the most favored by nature of any in the Union. There is no reason why, with a reasonable amount of enterprise and industry, this portion of the South should not be more attractive than any of our Northern counties. At present, however, the old traditions and habits engendered by slavery are too firmly fixed to be soon altered.

Few farmers manured their cultivated fields, and a yield of eight bushels of corn to the acre on uplands and of fifteen or twenty on lowlands was considered good. A bale (weighing 400 lbs.) of cotton could be produced from two or three acres without manure. Eight or ten bushels of wheat or oats was the average yield to the acre.[8]

In everything that pertains to agriculture, the South is at least fifty years behind the North.

The ploughs are generally of home manufacture, and by no possibility can they turn over the soil to a greater depth than four or five inches. The shares are narrow and but slightly curved, and very rarely is more than one horse used to drag it. When it is borne in mind that these ploughs are used on heavy clay land, it will readily be perceived that only a superficial culture could be possible.

The hoes in ordinary use were from two to three times as heavy as our light steel hoes in the North. They were of the same pattern and weight as were in use fifty years or more ago.

A field is cleared and cultivated as long as the land can produce anything. No manure of any kind is put on it, and when at last from simple exhaustion is not worth cultivating, it is thrown open to cattle and no more attention is paid to it. A fresh field is cleared in due time, and exhausted, shares the same fate. No pains are taken to save manure or to obtain it by composting, and even the wood ashes are thrown away where they can be of no service to the land. Under a free labor system, more careful cultivation and improved implements must be adopted.

It is useless to attempt to prove to the old farmers the advantages of deep ploughing and better cultivation. They were satisfied with the system of their grandfathers, and wanted nothing better. An Anderson farmer who had moved from Tennessee assured me that he was accustomed to plough deep and cultivate his land like Northern farmers, and that his crops were always better than his neighbors'. Still, they had not begun to follow his example.

In 1866 Anderson suffered in common with the rest of the state from a very severe drought. For eight or ten weeks in June, July and August, no rain fell. Cotton and corn were both cut short, and many would have starved had not the Government issued provisions the following year. Still, while this drought lasted, in some portions of the district rain fell every few days and there excellent crops were produced.

In conversation, many old slaveholders explained the cause of the wasteful system of agriculture which was so closely followed. Their main dependence was never on the produce of the lands. It was the increase of their slaves that was the basis of their wealth. The climate was healthy, and sickness very rarely prevailed among the negroes. By the labor of the older hands, enough was raised to feed everyone on the place, and from the sale of the cotton enough was bought to furnish clothes. Indeed on many plantations the women spun and wove all the clothing which the slaves wore.

Each year the number of slaves increased and so did their value, while the cost of maintenance was hardly felt. All surplus money was invested in more slaves, and thus a steady and secure profit was secured. If by chance a slaveholder was pressed for money, he could put a likely hand in the market and from his sale would get enough to relieve him. No man, at all familiar with the South or who will take a dispassionate view of the question of slavery, will deny the above statements.

In slave breeding the upper portion of South Carolina was beginning to rival Virginia. On the rice plantations and in the unhealthy plantations on the coast, a planter could afford to use up a hand in five or ten years. His place could readily be supplied from the healthy young hands to be found toward the mountains. It was not, therefore, the ambition of slave holders to raise fine crops of corn or cotton or to devote their energies to the development of manufactures and the raising of fruit. In every improvement of this sort there was danger to their previous institution which could only be prevented by maintaining themselves in the position the preceding generations had occupied.

With free labor, everything must be changed. Improved systems of agriculture must be adopted. Education must be diffused, and from education will follow all those blessings which freedom offers to those who will strive for them.

Morals and Religion

This is a theme for the theologian rather than the soldier. Still I cannot forego the opportunity of making a few, perhaps superficial remarks on the subject.

It was one of the first things which attracted my notice that nearly everybody was a devout church-goer and a member of some religious society. Men who on week days would get drunk, curse, fight and cheat would on Sundays be punctual in their attendance at church. I do not know as the South is peculiar in this respect, although I had never noticed the fact elsewhere.

The largest society in Anderson was the Baptist. It had quite a large brick church, comfortably furnished. It was without a seated pastor, its former one having resigned and taken to the law for a support. He was the Judge of the District Court and a very worthy man but, of course, a secessionist.

The Methodist Society was next to the Baptist in size and had a wood meeting house with a small steeple. The Presbyterians came next. Of their pastor I have already spoken. He was deformed because of a hump back, but was a man of a good deal of intellectual ability.

The Episcopal Society was the smallest and was without a seated minister. It had a pretty church, and its members were generally from the wealthiest portion of the community. During the time I was in Anderson, I went once to this church and as many times to the Baptist and Presbyterian.

The colored people were chiefly Baptist and worshipped by themselves. Before Emancipation they formed a part of the congregation at the regular church services but were frequently preached to at special services.

The church discipline of the Presbyterians was more strict than that of the other churches.

As to the general effect of religious teaching upon the community, it is not easy to judge. Every minister regarded slavery as a fixed, if not a divine, institution and never by word or deed threw a doubt upon its propriety. Their people had of course been educated with the same notion, and it was neither regarded as a sin to own slaves or to sell them.

The sacredness of the marriage relation among slaves was never regarded, although slaves were often married by the minister with as much solemnity as whites. They were "converted" by the same instrumentalities, baptized in the same manner, preached to as frequently, on removal to other places were recommended to fellowship, received the sacrament from the same vessels, and at death were buried with religious rites in the same manner as whites were.

But so perverted had become the consciences of the dominant race and so hardened were their hearts, they looked on with indifference to their wrongs, never hesitated for any but superficial reasons to sell their fellow beings, and would have severely punished anyone who attempted to teach them to read from the same Bible and Prayer-book. From my friend, Mr. [Andrew] Ramsay of Edgefield, I have heard of a very talented colored man who was even owned by a Baptist Society in Georgia and had been educated by it for the ministry, and went about preaching in the white churches to white congregations! At Edgefield C.H., where he once preached, he drew a very large audience and was generally acknowledged to be the superior of the regular minister who was a man of a good deal of ability.

And yet, in the face of the practice and profession of years, there have since Emancipation been many men who have pretended to believe in the arguments of "Ariel,"[9] which, as I understand, undertake to prove the negro a soulless animal—of course from the Bible.

If such is the case, what a monstrous farce have the Southern people enacted for years! If the negro has no soul, then here thousands of times has been enacted a worse ceremony than that attributed to Parker Pillsbury by his malignant enemies in the early days of the Anti-Slavery agitation—the baptism of a dog in the name of Father, Son, and Holy Ghost.

> "In religion what damned error but some sober brow
> Will bless it and approve it with a text
> Hiding the grossness with fair ornament."

When such is religion professed by a people, we can easily judge of their morals.

Cruelty to inferiors, pride, uncontrollable passions, and intemperance were the characteristics of many men of good social position and ability. Never before coming to South Carolina did I see drunkenness regarded as an amiable weakness of trifling moment. In their own families or in the presence of neighbors I have heard many men holding high positions joke and laugh about drunken sprees in which they have been engaged. But it is needless to enlarge upon this subject.

Where one race has uncontrolled power over another, it is easy to see the effect such power must have over the dominant class and the depressing influence it will produce in the weaker. When, therefore, it is said that the slaves were dishonest, were cruel to their own children, were careless of the marriage relation, and only induced to work through fear, it can easily be seen why they were so.

By their owners they were cheated out of personal freedom and the fruits of their labor. Many of them had suffered nothing but cruelty all their lives, and were naturally cruel to those who were weaker. They could not regard the marriage relation as sacred when any whim might separate husband from wife and parents from children. They could not but prefer idleness to work when the proceeds of their labor added nothing to their own comfort and improvement. When Charles Sumner pointed out these facts in his speech on the Barbarism of Slavery, the whole South was stirred up and sent forth an indignant denial. When Uncle Tom's Cabin was published, it was declared to be a malicious fiction.

But, I have yet to meet an officer of the Freedmen's Bureau who has not found ample proof of the severest charges brought against slavery. Many an old man have I seen whose wife and children were long ago sold from him to go further south to the cotton fields of Mississippi and Louisiana. Many an old woman has received food from the Bureau who years ago was brought from "Virginny" and separated from all that was dear to her. Many a child is there who has never known either parent and of whose existence no one but his owner cared.

There have been reported to me authentic instances of cruelty to slaves too horrible to be written, and so horrible that even the neighbors were <u>almost</u> moved to prosecute the perpetrator but didn't.

It is useless to repeat these stories now. They would not add to the enormity of the system itself, which allowed such barbarity. In fact, I have long thought that no stronger argument—if argument were needed to prove a self-evident truth—against slavery can be found than the first paragraph of the Negro Code adopted by the General Assembly of South Carolina in 1865. "The relation of husband and wife between persons of color is hereby established." There is the legal condemnation of the system by the state that stood forth as its foremost champion!

Nothing could be more forcible. A system existed which did not recognize the relationship of husband and wife. By any process of reasoning, could it be other than a barbarism?

There were, of course, many kind slave holders who under no circumstances would have separated families by sale. But upon their death, nothing could prevent that which they had so carefully avoided. Their slaves were chattels, and the law of course regarded no ties of family and kindred.

I have often been surprised at the real affection which seemed to exist between slave holders and their former slaves. Many instances have come to my notice where, after a few months absence, the freedmen have gone back to their old homes, trusting to their old owner's kindness to do right by them. There are many freedmen who still live in and have never left their old homes. While such instances of mutual affection and confidence are found, there are enough of the reverse to render every legal measure that can be adopted necessary to secure the freedmen their plainest rights.

Taxes

The Legislature of 1865 imposed a poll tax upon all persons between the ages of 18 or 21 and 60 except such as were manifestly incapable of making a support. This, of course, included the freedmen who were not then allowed to vote. However, as there was no military order prohibiting the collection of this tax, whenever I was asked if it should be paid, I said "Yes." My reason for this was that every law not in itself wrong ought to be obeyed. I objected to the law as unjust, but no harm could be done by obeying it, and it would have been wrong to have resisted it by such means as the freedmen possessed. I held, too, that as they were free they must perform the duties of free men, and seek by peaceable measures to increase their privileges and rights until they should have the same chance as the whites. When the Intendant of the Town called on me to know if I would interfere if they required the freedmen to do their share of road duty or pay a commutation, I told him I would not, but on behalf of the freedmen wrote a protest against the action of the Council in requiring persons to obey laws in the framing of which they had no voice, and requested that it be entered on the Journal of the Council, which was done.

Sooner than any of us could have expected, Congress gave the right of suffrage to the freedmen and made them amenable to the same laws.

Not only did colored people inquire if they ought to pay taxes but many white people did the same, some saying they had been deceived so much by their own people they did not know what to believe. Indeed, at Anderson I became sort of legal advisor to all the distressed poor people, and my advice was regarded with as much veneration as could have been that of the ablest lawyer. That it was good, I should not have the presumption to assert.

Public Men

The most prominent men of Anderson were Gov. Orr, Hon J. P. [Jacob Pinckney] Reed, Gen'l [James W.] Harrison, Judge Monroe, and Hon. R[obert] F. Simpson.

Gov. Orr's career in the House of Representatives is well known. He was a lukewarm secessionist, and never regarded secession as a peaceable measure. He was a member of the State Convention which passed the ordinance of secession. He raised a regiment of infantry and was commissioned Colonel but soon resigned it and was elected a member of the Confederate Congress representing the State in the Senate, I think. In Anderson he is often addressed by the title of Colonel.

At the close of the war, he was foremost in his endeavors to restore the Union, and at the first election was chosen Governor. [General Wade] Hampton had been nominated, but finding he would not be allowed to hold the office, he withdrew. This left Orr no opponent although if Hampton had run, Orr could not have been elected.

After his inauguration, he endeavored to suppress the outrages which were frequent, and recognized the necessity of such legislation as should secure justice to the freedmen. He favored schools for them, he advocated with much ingenuity the necessity for securing to them their Civil rights, and really did more than any South Carolinian to elevate them as a people.

His disabilities having been removed by Congress, he was elected a few weeks ago by the Republican Legislature as one of the Circuit Judges. I think during the term of his office as Governor he really accomplished more for the State than any man in it. He was a personal friend of Gen'l Sickles, and never sought or had any conflict with the military commanders. His course has rendered him unpopular to the white citizens generally, but time will prove the general correctness of his views and wisdom of his course.

Hon. J. P. Reed was the Solicitor of the Northern Circuit. He was a lawyer of much ability, and at different times was a candidate for Congress but was not elected. He was an ardent Secessionist, and while the 15th Me. was at Anderson, the officers got hold of some old papers containing his speeches which were full of wild assertions of the prowess of the South and the cowardice of the North. The expression which is most frequently quoted as having fallen from his lips is that he would wipe out with his pocket handkerchief all the blood that would be spilled in the war.

Unlike Gov. Orr, he had not the advantage of an acquaintance with the North and its public men. He signed the Ordinance of Secession but took no part in the war. In the summer of 1866 he made his first visit to New York, having gone there with a committee to solicit aid for the Blue Ridge Railroad. On his return, he made a public speech in the Court House to his fellow citizens in which he said, as I was informed by my landlord, Elijah Webb Esq., that he thought that if he could have seen New York before the war, he should not have favored secession so strongly.

Rather a humiliating confession for a man who ought to have been familiar with geography and statistics! He was the Intendant of the town when I first went to Anderson but was not re-elected. He was, I think, the Democratic candidate for Congress from his district.

Gen'l Harrison dates his title from militia days having, I think, taken no part in the war. He is an able lawyer and is now President of the Blue Ridge Railroad. He was, of course, a secessionist but I think has held no high political office.

Judge Monroe was one of the judges of the Superior Court until the new Constitution was adopted. He was not a strong secessionist and his reputation is chiefly local.

Hon. R. F. Simpson was, I think, a member of Congress some years ago. He is a farmer and signed the Secession Ordinance.

This District was the home of [John Caldwell] Calhoun, and with one of his intimate friends, Dr. O[zey] R. Broyles, I was well acquainted. The Doctor frequently came into my office and discussed the free labor question with a great deal of judgement and good sense. He did not share the fears of many persons that under the new system the blacks would not work. Of his own hands he always spoke in the highest terms. Of Calhoun he told me many anecdotes, and from his reports as well as those of others who had known him, I judge him to have been a man of singular goodness and integrity in private life. Certainly he was generally regarded with love and veneration. His political views and his remarkable ability are matters of history.

In connection with Calhoun, Dr. Broyles one day related the following story. They were both members of the Pendleton Agricultural Society, Dr. B[royles] being at the time referred to as its President. It was one of the rules that at their annual gathering the President himself or someone obtained by him should deliver an address. The Doctor chose to be his own orator, and took for his subject the question of Negro Slavery. He held that as each year the area of free labor was extended, it would be found impossible in a financial point of view to compete with it, hence slavery would gradually become extinct. He set fifty years as the limit of the institution. After he had concluded, Mr. Calhoun, who was sitting by him, congratulated him upon his address in the sentiments of which he concurred, but said he thought the time fixed by him was too short. He replied that on that point his strongest arguments had been adduced from a recent speech delivered by Calhoun. Dr. Broyles offered to lend me the address, but for some reason did not.

Another native of this district has achieved quite a reputation: Ex-Gov. Joe Brown of Georgia. A disciple of Calhoun and an ardent secessionist, since the war he has taken a firm stand on the platform of the Republican party and is now Chief Justice of Georgia.

Internal Improvements

A branch of the Greenville and Columbia R.R. runs to Anderson C.H., and furnishes the means of getting to the outside world.[10] It leaves the main trunk at Belton, twelve miles distant, and is not a model road. A great part of it is laid with shot rails tacked to stringers and these are much worn and quite unsafe. I do not know when the road was built, but it is safe to assume that the original rails are still in use.

From Anderson C.H. has been projected a road which shall cross the Alleghanies and by way of Knoxville unite Cincinnati with the sea. About thirty miles of this road are already built, and one or two tunnels have been excavated. The whole route is surveyed and the scheme is a good one.

The war compelled a suspension of the work, and the South is too poor to again undertake it. Gov. Scott in his message to the Legislature has urged its completion, and a bill has passed that body to loan it some of its bonds. It would be a fine thing for the State to have this road built and would do much towards developing its resources. In a military point of view, it would be of service to the United States.

Another railroad has been projected from Atlanta to Chester, S.C. which would pass through Anderson. Such a road would materially shorten the distance from the first named place to New York. If Southern capital, however, is required to build it, I am afraid this generation would pass without seeing it.

There are no canals, turnpikes, stages, or telegraphs. The roads are poor and the bridges shaky. In winter, some of the roads are almost impassible.

"Brown's Raid"

No account of the events which have taken place in Anderson would be complete without a reference to this celebrated—and to the upper districts of South Carolina—terrible raid.

I do not mean that it can compare with Sherman's March to the Sea or any of Sheridan's or Stoneman's raids, but every person from the "up country" can tell about it. As I understand it, immediately upon the surrender of Johnston's army to Sherman or perhaps a little before, a certain Gen'l [Simeon B.] Brown, with a brigade of cavalry from Michigan, East Tennessee, and Kentucky, was detached in pursuit of Jeff Davis. He passed through the upper districts of South Carolina and went into Georgia, but I do not know where he brought up. His troops appear to have been badly disciplined which is not surprising if they were composed of East Tennesseans.

On May day, 1865, the young people of Anderson were out a short distance from the village picnicking when the words reached them that "the Yankees had come." Now a Yankee had never before penetrated into this District except as an escaping prisoner, and with the knowledge the people had of Sherman's course, they not unnaturally regarded the aforesaid Yankees as a set of fiends. Then too, a depot of the Commissary Department had been here, and there was a branch of the Confederate Treasury also here—both attractive objective points. The young people made what haste they could into town and sheltered themselves in their homes. There was, of course, no force to oppose our troops and they at once took possession of the town. A lot of liquor which had been stored there was given up to them and the natural consequences followed. Stores were broken open and the goods distributed or appropriated indiscriminately. Safes were forced, money was stolen, jewelry was seized, and perishable property was destroyed. Horses were exchanged, good ones being taken and poor ones left. Provisions were appropriated and silver ware hunted up and kept.

They were at Anderson two or three days, and really conducted themselves outrageously. Two or three cases were reported where citizens had been suspended by the neck to make them confess where property was hidden. I do not think they found much in the Treasury Department except the plates on which Confederate notes were printed and the ordinary machinery for such work. They made no discrimination in their treatment of unionists or rebels. A strong union man named Taylor who kept a drug store had it broken open, his drugs were scattered to the winds, his safe was forced and his papers scattered, and he was left a ruined man.

In Abbeville they treated in a similar way a union man named McCalls. He had been entrusted with a quantity of gold belonging to some minor heirs, and it was confidently thought his well-known Union sentiments would protect him from molestation. It was, however, discovered in some way that he had this money secreted, and finally it was found and taken off. He followed the troops to Georgia and managed to get back part of it.

For such a raid as this I can see no excuse whatever. Certainly the United States did not raise troops to plunder unarmed citizens or carry on a system of outrageous pillage and robbery. The citizens used to say that it was the East Tennesseans who did the most stealing and that the "Michiganers" behaved pretty well. It was very likely the case that the former considered themselves as entitled to make up by robbery from other people what they had lost at the hands of their rebel neighbors. Still, every person who regards the good name of his country must condemn such conduct.

The first I heard of this raid was at Allston on my way to Anderson. It was not long after I reached there before I heard full particulars of it with more or less embellishments. To the credit of the negroes, be it said that in many instances they carried off into the woods and secreted valuable property of their owners which they returned safely after the raid was over. Many valuable horses particularly were saved by them.

I doubt if authentic reports of this raid were received by the War Department—at least before the muster out of the command, for no General who allowed such conduct in his troops would have escaped a Court Martial. But all the rail roads were cut, the mails had not been reestablished, and it was very difficult to communicate with the authorities at Washington. Even when I first went to Anderson, nearly a year later, we had but three mails a week, and it required a week to get a letter from the North. Outside of the State, very little, I think, is known of this marauding expedition so discreditable to those concerned in it and so injurious to the fame of our soldiers.

General Incidents

Under this head I shall refer to but a few events which were connected with the war in some way and of which there is plenty of corroborative testimony.

Of the treatment of Mr. Walker at Belton in the early days of the war I have already spoken. A similar, although worse, scene was enacted in Anderson village during the fall or winter of 1860, I think. A certain dentist named [John J.] Horn, I think, was suspected of holding Union sentiments or of being an abolitionist. He was also charged with inciting the slaves to insurrection. Here was reason enough for an application of Lynch Law in the eyes of the citizens, and accordingly he was taken by a vigilance committee to the Presbyterian burial ground, stripped, and flogged most severely. Prominent in this committee was Mr. [Crawford] Keyes who is alluded to above as having been on trial at Charleston before a Military Commission for the murder of the Maine soldiers when I went to Anderson. He was one of the prominent men of the District, eminently "respectable," and a good citizen. He was not thought the worse of for his conduct in this case, and some said it was his influence that prevented Horn from losing his life. After his flogging he was compelled to leave the State and went to Missouri. His brother-in-law was living in Anderson when I went there and from him as well as others I heard the above story. This brother-in-law and family obtained gov't transportation and followed Horn to Missouri while I was in Anderson.

The spot where the flogging took place was frequently pointed out to me.

Nathan McAllister, an outspoken Union man through the war, often received threatening letters and always went heavily armed. His pluck and his long residence in the District protected him.

Within the village of Anderson (That is its corporate limits) two United States horses were in August 1866 stolen from the man in whose charge they were while watering by two men whose names Col. Smith and all his officers had good reason for believing were known to the citizens, but they were not recaptured although immediate pursuit was made.

After a gross outrage had been committed in Pendleton upon a negro by a man named Keasler and some others, a gentleman named Sloan belonging to a very respectable family (his brother had been a classmate of Col. Smith at West Point) living there was in my office and affected to make light of the outrage because the negro had been accused of some theft. He then said that often before the war when any person, poor white or black (and generally the former for the owners looked out for the latter as he would for his other "stock") was suspected of stealing, the young men in the neighborhood would form "slicking parties" and go to his house and, calling him out, would give him a beating. He added, with what struck me as marvelous naiveté that corn cribs and smoke houses were seldom robbed in those days.

After I left Anderson, two ruffians rode into Anderson and amused themselves by shooting at Col. Smith and some of his soldiers. All of his horses were off and he could not attempt to chase down the men. The citizens turned out to try to assist him, but I think they failed at that time. However, the men were caught afterwards, if not then, and the older was tried by Military Commission and sentenced to seven years imprisonment at Fort Macon. The other one was a boy, and Col. S. did not press the prosecution against him. They intended to shoot Lieut. [Charles F.] Loshe, but he was away so they fired at Col. Smith instead.

These few incidents will serve to show how much respect was paid to laws and the proper administration of justice. Once, in Pendleton, a United States mail bag was opened by a mob because it was suspected of containing the N.Y. Tribune.

Free speech and free schools were, of course, unknown, and it was a penal offense to distribute abolition tracts or papers. One of the first titles in Pressley's Law of Magistrates treats of the laws on this subject.

I was on duty at Anderson six months. During that time I had learned much of the ways of the people, and had found my early ideas of the crime of slavery strengthened ten-fold. I had often felt depressed at the extent of the work before us, but never doubtful of final success in restoring not only the Union in its integrity but of infusing correct notions of government and liberty into the minds of the old slave holders and the whites generally and also of the freedmen.

On the 22nd day of September, 1866, I relinquished the charge of my office to Lieut. [G. P.] McDougall in order to proceed to Aiken for assignment to duty.

[*End of Part I*

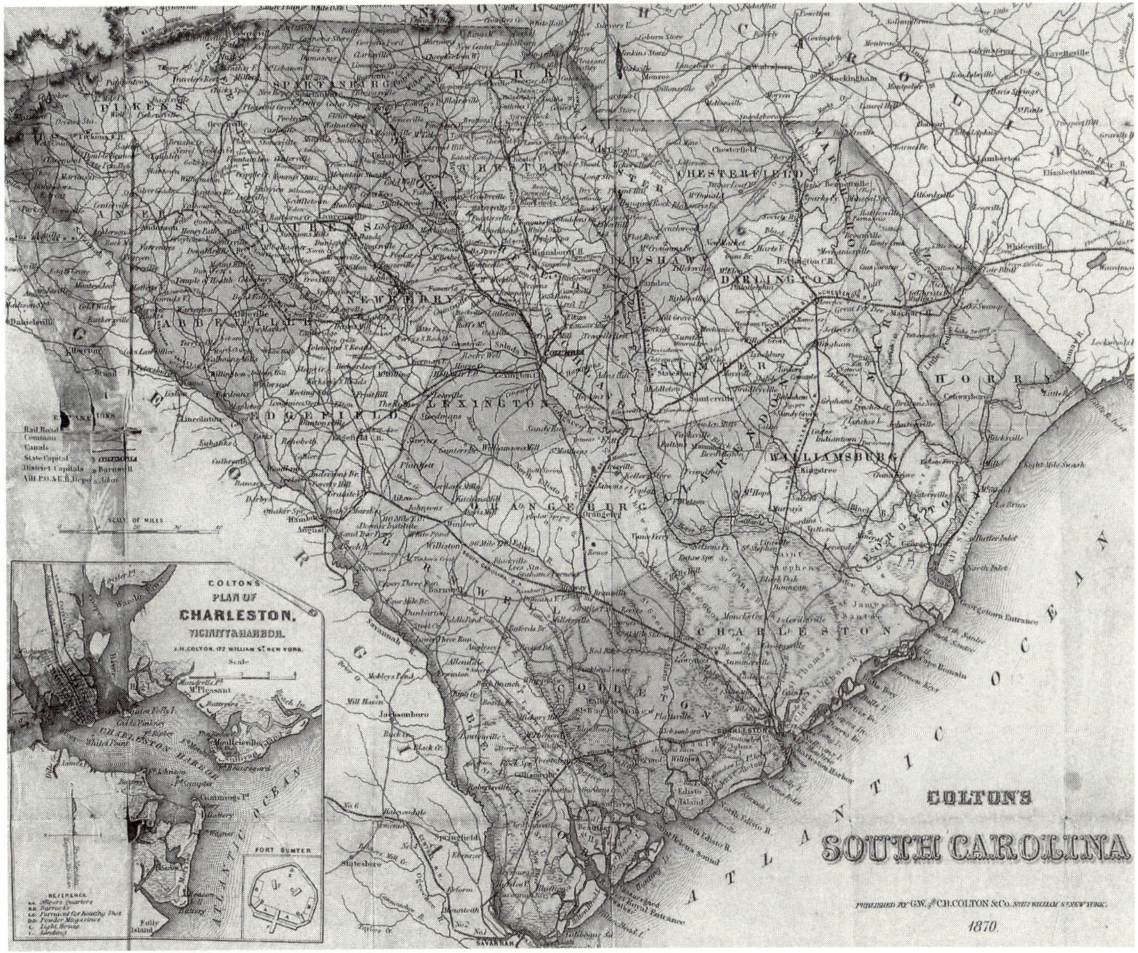

Map of South Carolina, 1870.
Courtesy of the South Caroliniana Library, University of South Carolina

Left: Mary Taylor before her marriage to William Stone.
Courtesy of the Stone Family Archives

Below: William Stone (right) and his older brother George as youths. George Stone died of wounds received during the Port Hudson campaign, May–June 1863.
Courtesy of the Stone Family Archives

Boyhood home of William Stone in Bolton, Massachusetts. William's father, Thomas Treadwell Stone, stands behind the fence on left. William's sisters, Martha and Mary, stand behind the hitching rail.

Courtesy of the Stone Family Archives

Reverend Thomas Treadwell Stone's Unitarian Meeting House in Bolton, Massachusetts, was built in 1793. Courtesy of the Bolton Historical Society

Above: Second Lieutenant William Stone in early 1863. Courtesy of the Stone Family Archives

William Stone, Boston, 1863, taken while Stone was on convalescent leave after the September 17, 1862, Battle of Antietam. Courtesy of the Stone Family Archives

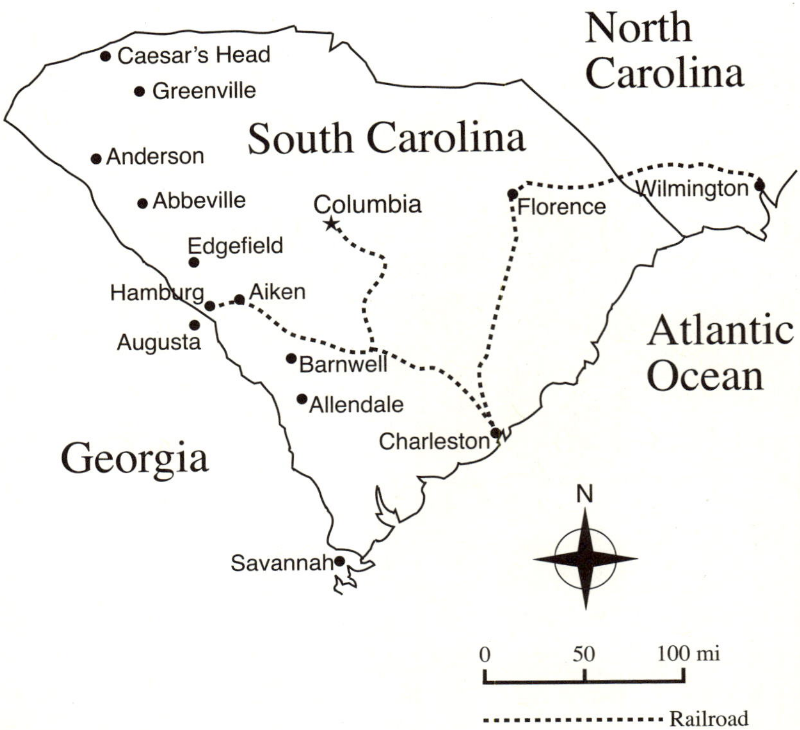

Map of William Ston's travels as a Freedmen's Bureau agent. Courtesy of Suzanne Stone Johnson

The residence of William Stone in Aiken, South Carolina, while he was on Freedmen's Bureau duty, circa 1867. Courtesy of the Stone Family Archives

This wooden sundial escaped destruction by Sherman's troops and continues to grace downtown Barnwell, South Carolina, to this day. Courtesy of the Stone Family Archives

The bell tower of the original Schofield School in Aiken, South Carolina, is located on the site of the present-day Martha Schofield Middle School. Courtesy of the Stone Family Archives

Left: South Carolina state historical marker at the site of the school. *Right:* William Stone, circa 1872, when he was assistant United States district attorney. Courtesy of the Stone Family Archives

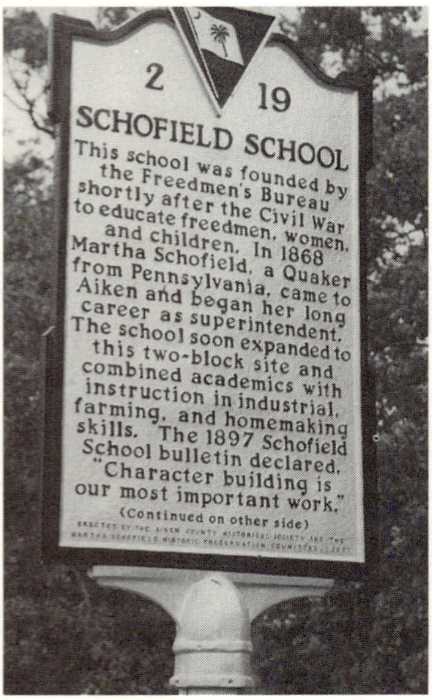

Left: William Stone, circa 1875, shortly before his appointment as attorney general of South Carolina. Courtesy of the Stone Family Archives

William Stone's commission as attorney general of South Carolina, signed by Governor Daniel H. Chamberlain, May 4, 1876. Courtesy of the Stone Family Archives

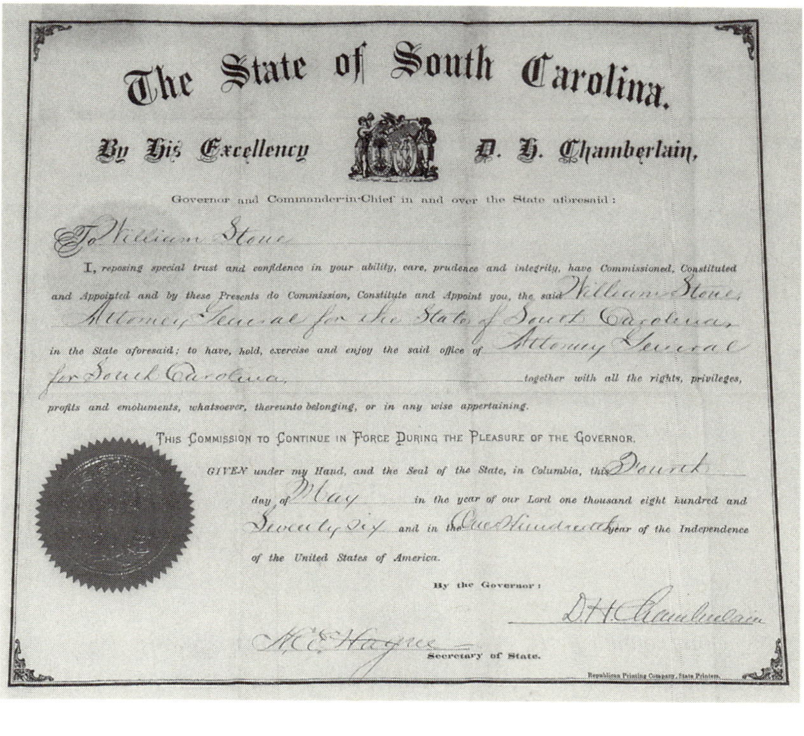

The State of South Carolina.

By His Excellency D. H. Chamberlain,

Governor and Commander-in-Chief in and over the State aforesaid:

To William Stone

I, *reposing special trust and confidence in your ability, care, prudence and integrity, have Commissioned, Constituted and Appointed and by these Presents do Commission, Constitute and Appoint you, the said* William Stone, Attorney General for the State of South Carolina, *in the State aforesaid; to have, hold, exercise and enjoy the said office of* Attorney General for South Carolina, *together with all the rights, privileges, profits and emoluments, whatsoever, thereunto belonging, or in any wise appertaining.*

THIS COMMISSION TO CONTINUE IN FORCE DURING THE PLEASURE OF THE GOVERNOR.

GIVEN under my Hand, and the Seal of the State, in Columbia, this Fourth *day of* May *in the year of our Lord one thousand eight hundred and* Seventy six *and in the* One Hundredth *year of the Independence of the United States of America.*

By the Governor:

D. H. Chamberlain

H. E. Hayne

Secretary of State.

Republican Printing Company, State Printers.

Mary Taylor Stone with her sons Alfred W. (left) and Herbert L. Stone, New York City, circa 1885. Courtesy of the Stone Family Archives

William Stone (standing), Mary Taylor Stone (seated nearest William), and friends in New Hampshire, circa 1895. Courtesy of the Stone Family Archives

Part II

On the 24th of September, 1866, I left Anderson for Aiken. The ride to Columbia was without any noteworthy incident. The bridge across Broad River at Allston had been completed, and we had no ferrying or staging as was the case when I went to Anderson. All along the railroad the effects of the drought were apparent in the withered corn and stunted cotton fields. Fields containing 100 acres of corn would hardly produce as many bushels, and the cotton was cut short a good deal. On the bottom lands the corn was generally good.

Spent the night in Columbia, and while there walked around the city some. I have already given my impressions of it. I wore my uniform and was much amused to see the scornful looks with which the young ladies regarded me. They seemed to think a Yankee polluted the very air with his presence.

On the following day I reached Aiken and, after having tea at the hotel, called on Gen'l [Benjamin P.] Runkle to whom I had been ordered to report. He informed me that only two murders of freedmen had been reported that day.

On the 26th I was assigned to duty as Sub-Assistant Commissioner for Edgefield District with office at Aiken.

Capt. E. R. Chase was also stationed here as Sub-Assistant commissioner for Barnwell District, although when I first reported he was off with a detachment of cavalry to investigate the report of an intended insurrection of negroes at Barnwell which, as usual, turned out to be utterly groundless.

Aiken was the Head Quarters of a Military Post which was at the time of my arrival, and until Sept. 12, 1868, commanded by Bvt. Major L[eicester].

Walker, 5th Cav. In addition to his duties as Sub-Assistant Commissioner, Capt. Chase was Judge of the Provost Court while it lasted.

For a few days after my arrival at Aiken I was engaged in the always disagreeable work of overhauling the papers left by my predecessor, Lt. McDougall, and in completing back work. All cases which were reported to me by freedmen were referred to the Provost Court for trial until the first of October, when an order was published by Gen. Sickles requiring their transfer to the Civil Courts.

This order was necessary from the fact that by the Act passed at the special session of the General Assembly, the freed people were placed upon the same footing as the whites as to their civil rights.

From that time until the passage of the Reconstruction Act of Mar. 2, 1867 by Congress, the military authorities and the officers of the Bureau were powerless to punish offences committed by or upon negroes or to secure to them their rights. During this interval I had not much to occupy my time in the office for every complainant had to be sent to a magistrate or attorney for redress.

On the 17th of October, Gen'l Runkle received an appointment as Major of the 45th Infantry, and on the following day he packed up and was ready to start for New York where he was to report for examination. On the 24th of October Major Walker assumed charge of Gen'l Runkle's office and continued to perform Bureau duty until Aug. 15, 1868.

So frequent had been the outrages in Edgefield, that in the latter part of October, Gen'l Sickles ordered another company of cavalry in command of Lieut. [James William] Walsh to report to Maj. Walker for duty therein. Lieut. Walsh was a very efficient officer and made several attempts to arrest the worst men in the District but without success. To aid in dividing crops, however, and to settle disputes relative thereto, he frequently sent out his soldiers who, without any particular authority but with the tacit consent of both parties, saw that justice was done.

In the latter part of December, I went myself to Edgefield and adjudicated one or two intricate cases in which one or both parties were represented by counsel. Upon the counsel for the employer asking by what authority I proposed to hear the case, I was somewhat at a loss for a satisfactory answer, although I claimed the right under the Act of Congress establishing the Freedmen's Bureau. Whether that answer would have been held as good by the Department Commander or the Assistant Commissioner is doubtful. Still, after a careful reading of the Act, strong arguments could be adduced in support of the claim. Be that as it may, no further opposition was made, and the case was decided adversely to the employer. Leave was asked and granted to enter a protest against my decision, but it was never drawn up and the hands were paid in accordance with it.

During all this time outrages were still frequent, and very few offenders were arrested by the civil authorities.[11] I have prepared an incomplete list which shows that no less than ten colored people were murdered in Edgefield District between June, 1866 and Feb., 1867, the murderers in every case but one or two being white men. Only three were tried and they were acquitted by the jury in the face of positive testimony. I doubt if there is a single instance since the war of an Edgefield jury convicting a white man of a crime committed against a negro no matter how strong the proof of his guilt.

In some cases the military authorities made arrests under the provisions of Gen'l Order No. 44 Headquarters of the Army dated July 6th, 1866 which required Department, District, and Post Commanders in the states lately in rebellion to arrest all persons charged with the commission of crimes in cases where the civil authorities had failed, neglected, or were unable to bring such parties to trial, and to detain them in military custody until such time as a proper judicial tribunal might be ready and willing to try them.

Such being the condition of things, a Bureau officer being comparatively powerless to do anything for the freedmen and the civil authorities being independent of military control, I urged in two or three reports the withdrawal of officers doing Bureau duty at military posts and the assignment of an officer of the Post for such duty which then was merely nominal. But to my suggestions no attention was paid, so I still remained at Aiken.

Early in January, 1867, I received an appointment in the 45th Infantry as First Lieutenant and went on to New York for examination. Having passed that satisfactorily, I was ordered to return to Aiken and resume my duties. At this time the indications were that the Bureau would no longer be a useless part of Government furniture.

The elections of 1866 had been carried by heavy majorities by the Republican party, and Congress was more than two thirds on that side. The reports from all sources from the South were such as required Congressional action, and it was evident that some plan would be adopted by which it would be again put practically under martial law. On the 2nd of

March, 1867, the original Reconstruction bill was passed, dividing the South into Military Districts commanded by General Officers who should under the authority of the United States exercise all powers necessary to the protection of persons and property.

South Carolina was included with North Carolina in the Second Military District, to the command of which Gen'l Sickles was assigned.

In March, 1867, Maj. [Erastus W.] Everson, Inspector on Gen'l Scott's staff, visited here and with him I went to Edgefield C.H. The Civil Court was in session and from what we saw and learned from reliable persons we were convinced that it would be impossible for freedmen to attempt to secure their rights through it. On the 26th of March, I made a report stating the uselessness of expecting that freedmen could obtain justice before the civil courts of Edgefield, and recommended the appointment of a Provost Court.

This report Maj. Walker approved and forwarded to Gen'l Scott, and at the same time as Post Commander wrote to Gen'l Sickles on the subject. The result was that on the 18th of April a Provost Court was appointed for the Post—then embracing Edgefield and Barnwell Counties—composed of 2nd Lt. E. [Edward] P. Doherty, 5th Cavalry, A[ndrew] Ramsay, Esq., and myself. By virtue of rank I was the presiding officer. A more detailed account of the proceedings of this court will be given hereafter.

On the 27th of November, 1867, I was ordered to assume charge of Barnwell District as well as Edgefield, as Capt. Chase had been mustered out of service at his own request. The additional responsibility did not add much to my labors for I had my office still at Aiken and very little trouble had occurred in Barnwell. I made two journeys there, however, with small detachments, once in January to distribute some clothing to destitute people, and again in March to distribute provisions and clothing.

On the 23rd of March I was relieved of the charge of Barnwell district by Mr. M. A. Nuland, formerly Captain 33rd U.S. Colored Troops and originally of the First Mass. Infantry. He continued in charge until the summer of 1868 when he was elected clerk of the Court of Common Pleas and General Sessions of that District (or County).

It had become apparent early in the year that it would be necessary for the Government to take measures to relieve the suffering which was inevitable by reason of the drought of the preceding summer. Hundreds of families were without three months supply of food, and were without means of procuring it. The civil authorities could take care of but few paupers, and unless the Government should provide for the mass of poor people, their condition would have been terrible. The action of Congress in appropriating $500,000 of the Freedmen's Bureau Fund for the purchase of food to relieve the destitution there threw an immense amount of work on the officers of the Bureau. My share in this work will be referred to hereafter.

It will be difficult to follow in chronological sequence the various duties which devolved on me during the very busy year of 1867 and the first half of 1868. I will, therefore, treat of them under their proper heads. Before doing this, however, I will briefly state what records were required to be kept and what reports made by officers of the Bureau. This will apply as well to my office at Anderson as the one at Aiken. It is hardly necessary to explain the method of keeping the records as that is explained fully in a pamphlet published by the Adjutant General of the Army and in the Manual for Officers of the Bureau. They were:

1. Record of Letters Received and Endorsement Book in which was entered a synopsis of every official letter received and the endorsements thereon in full.
2. Record of Letters Sent containing an exact copy of every official letter written and sent out.
3. Record of Complaints in which all complaints were briefly entered and the action taken on them noted. At Aiken I did not keep this book as I had no power as a Bureau officer to adjudicate cases.

The Reports were: 1. Report of Freedmen and Refugees to whom medicines, clothing, and rations were issued. 2. Report of Lands Held by Bureau Officers whether abandoned or confiscated. 3. Report of Condition of Freedmen and operations of office. 4. Report on Education giving number of schools, names of teachers, etc. This was not required until 1868. 5. Report of persons employed and property hired. 6. Report of Officers and civilians on duty in district. 7. Return of property belonging to Bureau. 8. Return of clothing belonging to Quartermaster's Dept. 9. Quarterly statements of property. All of the reports but the quarterly statements are required to be made monthly.

Schools

At Aiken a school was opened a few days after I came here by Mr. A. M. Bigelow who was a young Methodist minister from somewhere in Mass. sent out by the Freedmen's Union Commission. He had been here only one or two nights when a party of young men went to the house of Mrs. Davenir, a respectable colored woman, where he boarded, and with curses and threats compelled him to sign an agreement to leave Aiken by the first train. After the party had succeeded in this, they left. By and by he sent a messenger to Gen'l Runkle's house, which was quite near, and told him of his resolution. He sent for him to come over, and immediately sent his servant to Camp to inform Maj. Walker of the affair. Mr. Bigelow was firm in his determination to go, although urged to remain at Gen'l Runkle's house, if necessary. As the train went at any early hour, he was off before daylight.

This was on the 12th of October. Gen'l Runkle made a report of the case, and sent Capt. Chase with it to Gen'l Scott and every effort was made by the military authorities to find out who the actors in this outrageous affair were but all to no purpose. The citizens in private conversation discountenanced the deed, but publicly took no action to express their abhorrence of it, and the civil authorities made no effort that I ever knew of to find out the rioters. Military control had but just been withdrawn and the fall elections had not taken place, so the unruly young men thought they could with safety and honor (!) drive off an unprotected man guilty of no crime, who in the exercise not only of his rights as an American citizen but of a praiseworthy occupation, came to Aiken to teach the freed children how to read and write!

The suspicions of the officers rested on several young men accounted to be respectable, but it would be useless to repeat their names here as no positive proof was obtained against them.

On the 19th of October the school was reopened by a Mr. Hammond, who had been sent here from Columbia and who remained here about three weeks. In December, my sister [Martha Stone] took charge of the school and taught here until June, 1868, Miss Stevens of Philadelphia being with her during the school year ending at that time. The school was quite large, numbering generally somewhat over one hundred scholars. In 1867 the school was taught in the colored Methodist Church, a rough building very cold in winter and the reverse in summer. It was without glass windows, and at the North would not have passed for a good barn.

During the winter of 1867–8 a frame building was hired by the Bureau for a school house but it was not large enough and in no way appropriate. When the warm weather came, Miss Stevens took her scholars to the Methodist Church, leaving my sister with hers in the hired building. In addition to this school, Mrs. Storey, an intelligent colored woman, has taught a private school here for two or three years. Her school generally numbered from 10 to 15 scholars.

At present (September 1868), a movement is on foot to build a school house here, but it is doubtful if a free school is taught here next year.[12] The people are too poor to hire a teacher, and the Freedmen's Union Commission declines to send out one. The State is not yet in a condition to support a system of free schools as by the Constitution of the State it is required to do. At Edgefield C.H. a school was taught when I first came here by a Mr. Laurence Cain, an intelligent colored man, formerly a slave of Maj. [James A.] Carwile, Commissioner in Equity of Edgefield District. He was almost white and accompanied one of his owner's family to the war. He was at one time taken prisoner and passed for a rebel soldier and was exchanged as such, I think. He relied upon the pay received from the scholars for his support. A Mr. Green also taught a private school for some time, but last year they united and kept one school. I visited it two or three times and found that the scholars had really made great progress.

In April, 1868 Mr. Cain was elected a member of the lower House of the General Assembly, and Mr. Green kept on with the school. This summer he has been assisted by payments from the Salem, Mass. Freedmen's Aid Society to the amount of thirty or forty dollars. I doubt if a Northern teacher could have taught at Edgefield, so great is the bitterness there against such persons, but these colored men were well known and generally liked and were never interfered with.

They have really accomplished a great deal and their scholars are further advanced than those in the other schools which have reported to me. There is no school house owned by the freedmen at Edgefield, and the one in use serves also as a meeting house on Sunday and for meetings of the Republican Club in the evening.

A man named Dreyspring endeavored to get up a school at Storm Branch Meeting House, three miles from Hamburg, in the fall of 1866, but he met with little encouragement and soon gave it up. I have heard nothing from him since. An attempt was made last year to carry on a day school there, but that also failed owing to the poverty of the people and the distance most of them lived from it.

This church is on the road from Barnwell to Augusta near a small stream, but a fine spring is close at hand and to this fact must be attributed its location for only one house is within a quarter mile or more of it. It is,

I believe, owned by the freedmen, having been given to them wholly or in part by a Mr. Dunbar on whose land it is. It is quite well built, has good seats, is whitewashed, and is quite as good as many white churches in this country. It is used by the Baptists, I think.

In the summer of 1867 a school was established at Summer Hill or Sleepy Hollow (the pupils came from the Hill to the school house in the Hollow), and taught for a year by a colored man named Gardner. He is at present a member of the lower house of the General Assembly. He had a very good school which averaged about thirty scholars. They paid for their own tuition.

The school house was a building which had been used as a laboratory to a distillery at Sleepy Hollow (2 miles from Hamburg) built during the war for the rebel Government by W. F. Howells, Navy Agent and I think a brother-in-law of Jeff Davis. This property was first seized by a Treasury agent, and afterwards taken possession of by me for the use of the Bureau and is reported on my Report of Lands. The laboratory made a very good school house, and I was instructed by Gen'l Scott to allow its being used for that purpose.

In the latter part of March, 1868, I found that a freedmen's school had been started in Graniteville. The teacher, Mr. John R. Sneed, had been a rebel soldier and lost his left leg at the Battle of Chickamauga. The school had been started as a branch of the Graniteville Academy in order that the latter might derive some advantage from the Leate school fund, the disbursement of which to any but free schools open to all children Gen'l [Edward Richard Spragg] Canby had forbidden. Under no circumstances could any be disbursed until a State system of free schools had been adopted. Fearing that in this matter there was much risk, the principal of the Academy told Mr. Sneed that he could not employ him after the first of April. Mr. Sneed had become interested in the school and did not wish to have it discontinued, so through Rev. Mr. Pickett (whose name is referred to in the first part) he sought aid from the Bureau.

I went in a few days to Graniteville and had a meeting of the colored people and urged them to employ Mr. Sneed and pay him themselves. This they promised to do but, as I anticipated, they failed to keep up to their agreement. Accordingly I advised Mr. Sneed to close the school entirely. This, however, he did not do. In the meantime I wrote to Rev. Mr. Willsen, President of the Salem, Mass. F.A. Society and set forth the condition of the school with some hope of getting aid for it.

In this I was more than successful. Two appropriations of fifty dollars each were voted for me to use for schools which enabled me to give twenty dollars to Mr. Sneed in May and June, and thus continue the school. Since then this Society has most generously undertaken to pay him twenty five dollars per month for October, November, and December, besides having paid him at the same rate for his services as teacher in July, August, and September.

The school was first taught in a very good meeting house built of hewn logs owned by the colored people, but this building was burned one night, in all probability because it had been used for a Republican meeting. After this, Mr. [Nooley?], one of the members of the lower house of the General Assembly, allowed the use of an old building of his for a school, and here Mr. Sneed now teaches.

This building was once used in connection with hat manufactory and is entirely unfit for its present use. The only seats are rough boards around the room, but here are from thirty five to fifty scholars daily, all eager to learn and making good progress in their studies. It speaks well for the interest not only of the scholars but also of Mr. Sneed that they should be willing to put up with such inconveniences for the sake of learning. I doubt if any set of white children in similar circumstances would have made greater progress than Mr. Sneed's scholars. The same is true I think of most colored scholars. If the poor whites of the South do not show soon such a desire for acquiring knowledge as is manifested by the colored people, they will in a few years find themselves far behind them in intelligence and the esteem of their neighbors.

Although every colored school is open to white children, I have not known one who has availed himself of the privilege of attending it owing to the extreme prejudice which exists against the blacks.

Yet colored and white children are allowed to play together with impunity and no objection is made to it. It will take many years to put new notions on this subject into the heads of the people of the South. It was no small task at the North, and has not yet been accomplished there.

For some months a small school has been in operation at the Ridge near Cloud's Creek, once one of the worst portions of Edgefield District. In the midst of an old field, a quarter of a mile or more from the road or from other houses, is the school house, a rough building made of pine slabs with the usual board shingles covering. It contains two rooms, one of which is the school room. Here on benches in keeping with the rest of this establishment, I found one day in March 1868, some 12 to 15 little boys and girls hard at work over their spelling books. The teacher was a young mulatto woman who had been born free. She had but little education herself; still she could teach beginners how to read and write. She had first taught at another place, but owing to some threats made against the school, moved to the place described above. The simple fact that anything called a freedmen's school could be taught in that neighborhood was an encouraging one of itself, and as the people were very poor and no one else could be found to carry on a large one, I sent the teacher sixteen dollars from the money sent me by the Salem F.A. Society.

At Hamburg, two or three attempts were made to have a school, but as the people were all poor and could not pay the teachers and no aid could be obtained from Northern societies, they all failed after a short trial. At no place was there more need of a school of the right sort, but it was impossible to have one.

Besides the day schools referred to, there were a good many Sunday Schools all of which were of some benefit to the freed people. Then too, by these means the minds of the whites became accustomed to the idea of teaching the blacks, and to that extent the old prejudices were overcome.

As an illustration of this prejudice, my friend, Mr. Ramsay, one day in a public speech referred to the statement made to him by Gov. [Milledge L.] Bonham that when he first saw the little negro children leaving his yard with their books to go to school, it used to make him "mad." Soon, however, he ceased to notice them, and even advocated their being educated. So much for the effect of time and habit in eradicating prejudice.

Of the schools in Barnwell, I know but little. There were no public ones there, although at different places there were small private ones and many Sunday Schools.

In the spring of 1868, I received from the American Tract Society of Boston a box containing nearly five hundred "Lincoln" Primers, First and Second Readers, and Spelling Books for distribution. These were given to people connected with day or Sunday Schools in different portions of my District and were very acceptable. They taught a doctrine which I could not accept, but which nevertheless, was that held by the majority of the people here, and they could not fail to do much good. In many places the white citizens did a great deal to encourage schools and at the Sunday Schools particularly, acted as teachers.

Administration of Justice

I have already alluded to the neglect of the civil courts of Edgefield to do justice to the freedmen, and the failure of the civil authorities to bring criminals to justice for the offences committed against them. This neglect can be attributed to no fault of the Judges, for they were generally good men who charged the juries with fairness and endeavored to have them render correct verdicts. But it was of little use for, in spite of the weight of evidence, juries would not convict whites for crimes against negroes. There was a radical defect in the popular understanding which rendered this sort of thing possible. As an instance of how little regard was paid to their oaths by an Edgefield jury, I will mention their action on cases submitted to them at the last March term (1868) of the Superior Court.

Cases were called and no defense would be set up against the claims of the plaintiffs, except that the debt was contracted before the war and was directly or indirectly based upon slave property. The judge repeatedly charged the jury to find for the plaintiff for the full amount claimed, but instead of so doing it would retire, calculate the amount of the debt—principal and interest—and divide it by four or some other number and render a judgement for that amount. It was not pretended that these judgements were in accordance with law but the jury, taking the condition of the country into consideration not on the technical plea of an attorney "Failure of Consideration," but for public convenience and fancied equity, gave judgement accordingly. Several such judgements were given in the course of one afternoon while I was in the court room. But there was another jury at the same court to which during the absence of the one first spoken of, other cases of a like character were submitted. That jury found judgements in accordance with law until two members on it were challenged and their places supplied by others when it, too, followed the example of the first.

From this it will be seen that the correctness of the verdict of one jury was due to the presence of two men who swayed the other ten. While they remained on the jury, it was the aim of the lawyers to have cases in which they represented the plaintiff referred to one jury, and those in which they represented the defendant referred to the other. It was not unusual for them to address the two juries with arguments directly opposed to each other. And yet there were many persons who regarded these jurymen who, in defiance of their oaths and against the express terms of the law, rendered these illegal judgements as public benefactors!

I do not know of anything which could so soon bring the whole system of English and American jurisprudence into discredit as such verdicts. One may well ask where is the fancied purity of jury trials if juries render verdicts not according to law and evidence, but according to their own notions of public equity.

It may be said that these verdicts were given in civil and not in criminal cases, but would men who disregarded their sacred obligations in one class of case observe them in another?

The lawyers were, of course, indignant as a class and the judge, I think, pronounced the conduct of the juries "monstrous." To such juries, however, must the security of property and the punishment of criminals be entrusted!

In Barnwell district no such anomaly was ever presented to my knowledge. There the juries generally rendered as correct verdicts as could be looked for, and freedmen were generally sure of protection from their hands. It was with some regret, therefore, that the military officers here found that Gen'l Sickles had classed the civil courts of Barnwell with those of Edgefield in his order establishing a Provost Court because it had become apparent that justice to the freedmen could not be obtained in the civil courts within the military post of Aiken. The members of the bar at Barnwell were naturally inclined to be indignant at such a statement. However, the order was soon after changed and the objectionable words were omitted. I am sure that I never intentionally asserted that the civil courts of Barnwell would not do justice to the freedmen, for I entertained the contrary opinion. But of Edgefield, I did frequently in official reports make such assertions and I then thought, and now think they were true.

Indeed none of the lawyers at Barnwell expressed surprise at the applicability of Gen'l Sickles words to Edgefield, for they said it had always been a turbulent District and noted for the number of murders which had been committed there. It was in the summer of 1868 that the Clerk of the Court at Edgefield, S. Harrison, Esq., told me that for years there was never a session of the Superior Court at which one or two murder cases were not tried.

My friend, Mr. Ramsay, who has lived in the District for nearly thirty years, told his associates of the Provost Court of at least twenty murders committed there within his recollection and besides those, there were many which he could not recall to mind. One of the prominent men of that District, Mr. Geo. D. Tillman, was a few years since tried for the murder of a man named Christian in a gambling house, and was convicted of manslaughter. He was sentenced to imprisonment for a term of years, and served it out wholly or in part in Edgefield jail. In 1866 he represented his District in the upper house of the General Assembly!

The District Court was organized, and Hon. John E. Bacon was the Judge. He was before the war Secretary of Legation to his father-in-law, Ex. Gov. [Francis W.] Pickens, at the Court of St. Petersburg, and is a man of good ability and liberal views. But the Provost Court took nearly all the business which would have gone to his, and it was therefore of little account.

The magistrates had jurisdiction in all suits up to twenty dollars but could not hear criminal cases. They were often inefficient and could do little towards protecting the freedmen in their rights. Under the new constitution they are to be chosen by the people (before they were appointed by the Governor for four years, I think) and have jurisdiction in cases to the amount of one hundred dollars, and can also try petty offences. They will be the officers on whom the freedmen especially must rely for advice and assistance when this Bureau is discontinued, and if they are good men can do a great deal of good.

Provost Court

A Provost Court for the Military Post of Aiken having been established by order from Headquarters, 2nd Military District dated April 18, 1867, consisting of myself as President, and Lieut. [Edward P.?] Doherty and A. Ramsay, Esq. of Edgefield as associates, it was ordered to meet on the 6th of May at Edgefield. I was not able to reach Edgefield the 6th, but the following day I was there and the Court was organized, I. N. Teague, Esq. being appointed Clerk.

The Court had jurisdiction of any case to which a person of color was party except capital crimes. A record of its proceedings was kept and submitted to the Post Commander for approval. Sentences imposing fines exceeding one hundred dollars or imprisonment were forwarded to District Headquarters for approval.

The Post Commander referred cases to the Court for trial, and for a short time caused the arrest of persons accused of crimes, and the summoning of witnesses to be done by his troops but as the business increased, the civil officers were required to do this.

After a session at Edgefield, sessions were held at Aiken and Barnwell C.H. At Edgefield we met at the camp of Co. "L" 5th Cav. where a tent was provided for our accommodation. At Aiken my office was the Court room, and at Barnwell C.H., Mr. Myers, an attorney, placed a room at our service. At these three sessions, very little business was transacted. Before the second session, Lieut. Doherty had been relieved in consequence of a promotion which carried him to another Company. Mr. Ramsay and I, therefore, acted as Judges, the examination of witnesses falling to me and the swearing of them to him. This division of labor was maintained as long as the Court lasted.

The relief of Lieut. Doherty rendered another Associate necessary, and Mr. Teague was appointed to the vacant place by orders from Headquarters of the District dated June 18, 1867. The same orders extended the jurisdiction of the Court to any cases not capital which might be referred to it by the Post Commander.

Under the new order, the Court met on the 18th of July at Edgefield and, at the solicitation of the members of the bar and by the advice of Messrs Ramsay and Teague, we held the session at the Court House which the Commissioners of Public Buildings kindly offered us. Chas. Edmondston, Esq. was appointed Clerk. No changes occurred in the organization of the Court after this time.

As the Provost Court met frequently, gave summary judgements, and enforced execution promptly, it was soon resorted to by whites as well as blacks, and its business increased rapidly. It sentenced several whites for crimes committed against negroes, and it was not long before they ceased almost entirely. At the last terms of the Court, a case of assault and battery or other outrage upon a negro was a rarity.

The Court met once in three or four weeks for a session of five or six days at Edgefield C.H., Aiken, or Barnwell C.H. At Aiken, the Town Council offered the use of the Town Hall for its sessions and at Barnwell—as there was no Court House—Sherman's forces having destroyed it—the Presbyterian Church was hired for a few terms and was afterwards tendered the Court free of charge.

Lawyers practiced before it as before the other Courts and, as far as possible, the rules of practice of the civil courts were followed. Magistrates issued warrants returnable to the Provost Court, and bound over prisoners and witnesses to attend it. In civil cases the proceedings were upon petitions similar to those adopted for the District Court of the State. Indictments were preferred as in Courts-Martial in the form of Charges and Specifications.

Sheriffs and all other civil officers were required to obey its orders when approved by the Post Commander.

If a case came up in which there was no counsel, the Court conducted the examination of witnesses, the President of the Court performing in this respect the duties of a Judge Advocate before a Court Martial. From the organization of the Court to its discontinuance, over seven hundred cases were referred to it, most of which were adjudicated.

On the 30th of September, 1867, a circular was published by Gen'l Canby limiting the jurisdiction of the court to causes of action within three hundred dollars, and prohibiting it when the title to land was involved. On the 6th of February, 1868 its jurisdiction was still further curtailed, being confined chiefly to questions involving rights under military orders. After that date very few new cases arose.

In June the last session of the Court was held at Aiken, and on the 13th of July was abolished, the State having been restored to its proper relation to the General Government.

Although none of the members of the Court were lawyers by profession, still the lawyers generally spoke of our decisions as being correct, and in very few cases were the proceedings disapproved. While sitting on the Court, I was, of course, compelled to devote as much of my spare time as possible to the study of law but of course acquired only superficial knowledge of it.

As the business of the Court increased and new questions arose, I saw under what great disadvantages we labored in having no legal training and no knowledge of precedents. Still the members of the bar were very kind to us, and never hesitated to give the Court information when called upon, and here I can re-iterate, what I have frequently expressed, my personal and official obligations to nearly all of them for their uniform kindness and courtesy. As a body, they showed a liberality of thought which I had not before met with and, although all of them differed from me in political opinion, still they have never shown me anything but kindness and goodwill. Could they have acted as juries in cases where freedmen were concerned, I am confident that they would have decided them justly.

If they objected to military tribunals, so did the Court, but we were sorry for the necessity which created it. For my own part, I should never again wish to sit upon such a Court or see such a one established unless it were a military necessity. Such a necessity, I hope, will never again exist in this country.

It was our endeavor to deviate as little as possible from the established practice of civil courts, and to soften the arbitrariness of military rule. I am sure we did not absolutely fail in this, and that we enjoyed to a great degree the confidence of the people.

When it was proposed by Maj. Walker to confine the sitting of the Court to Aiken, petitions were drawn up both at Edgefield and Barnwell C.H., praying that we still might be allowed to meet at those places. These petitions were signed by almost every, if not every lawyer at those places and had the desired effect.

The experience I gained while in this Court and the opportunity it gave me for acquiring information in an entirely new field was most valuable, and while on it I was enabled to render more effectual service to the freedmen than in any other position which I have occupied since being in the Bureau.

When it was abolished, the records of proceedings covered more than a thousand pages, and the original papers made a heavy bundle. Everything pertaining to it was packed up and sent to Headquarters of the District. Every month, I had to make a report of the cases tried and the money received and spent on account of the Court.

The members were paid four dollars per day while on duty. The Clerk was paid three dollars per day. Executions to the amount of over two thousand dollars were left in the hands of the Sheriffs when it was abolished.

In order to prevent any dispute as to the validity of the judgements of the Provost Courts and Military Tribunals, and to protect the members from vexatious suits which might be instituted because of them, I made a report on the 16th of June recommending that an Act of the General Assembly should be passed ratifying the judgements of Provost Courts and forbidding prosecutions on account of services rendered under their orders. I do not know as yet whether this has been done.

Issue of Rations

In March, the issue of rations to destitute freed people began. At the first, only a few old and destitute people received anything, but soon the cry for food became general. I went to Edgefield and issued a quantity there and, before Capt. Nuland took charge of Barnwell District, issued a supply there.

Early in April, at the request of J. M. Norris, Esq. I visited the Ridge to investigate the condition of the poor people in that vicinity. I learned that there were many families absolutely without the means of supporting life until another harvest could be gathered. Mr. Norris, whom I had found an honest, public spirited man and one who took a serious and active interest in educating the freedmen, offered to superintend the distribution of supplies if any could be obtained. During the winter and spring, various charitable associations had been formed at the North designed to aid by a distribution of money and provisions the destitute people throughout the South. One of these, the Southern Famine Relief Association used the Bureau as its medium for distribution. At my suggestion, Mr. Norris made an application for corn from this association, and on the 23rd of April fifty sacks (100 bushs.) of corn was received from it to be given to the poor without regard to past condition or color.

As soon as possible, Mr. Norris came for this corn and issued it, I have every reason to believe, with great fairness and good judgement. He received afterwards one hundred bushels more, (and perhaps a larger quantity) which he also issued. He made a full report to me of the quantity issued to each destitute person or family. The destitution in that portion of the District was very great. I was assured that not more than two or three planters within a radius of ten miles raised enough corn to supply their needs until harvest. Maj. Tillman Watson, an excellent planter told me that he would have to buy corn for the first time in forty years. In the adjoining District of Lexington, where the land was not so good as in Edgefield, and in the portion which was called the "chincopin country," the destitution was greater.

As Aiken was the nearest railroad station, although twenty five miles distant, supplies for that section came to a Dr. Kunce in my care. So great was the distance which these supplies had to be hauled, a portion of the corn had to be given for having it done. Dr. Kunce, like Mr. Norris, rendered full report of the issues which he made.

For Edgefield C.H., I drew rations on Provision Returns. The Post Commissary was ordered to issue on them, and Maj. Walker furnished the transportation for them to the camp of Co. "L" 5th Cav. at Edgefield, eighteen miles distant over a sandy, rough road. There a man detailed for the purpose made the issues on lists prepared by me for the purpose. The issues were made nearly every week, and often I rode up from Aiken to superintend them. In the roadside in front of the camp on ration days would be seen a motley collection of people of all ages, color, and condition, nearly, dressed in garments of every hue, and ragged enough for a Falstaffean army. Some were crippled with age and rheumatism, some were sickly, some were deserted by their husbands and, I am sorry to say, some were most skillful cheats. I tried hard to give to none who were not actually in want, but some would find a way to get rations in spite of all my precautions. I required everyone to bring a certificate from responsible persons, but I found this was no protection, and finally I had to guess at the truths of each one's story after a close examination. It was not until August that I ceased to issue rations here. From some Northern Society, six hundred bushels of corn were sent to prominent citizens at Edgefield to distribute. This was taken charge of by the Commissioners of the Poor, and issued in different parts of the District under their directions. I have no doubt they distributed it faithfully.

At Aiken, the issue of rations and corn was no easy task. Maj. Walker drew the provisions which were required for the needy people here and in this neighborhood on Provision Returns, but the Commissary of the Post was ordered to make the issue.

On the days on which issues were to be made came the poor people from miles around for provisions. A few would come with wagons borrowed for the purpose, and a few would ride old broken-down horses. The greater number, however, would walk. The duty of investigating the circumstances of each applicant devolved upon me, and it was often difficult to tell who were really worthy and who were not. Lists were prepared, however, containing sometimes as many as three hundred names of whites and one hundred and fifty or two hundred blacks. As each applicant applied, his name was checked, the amount issued being stated opposite it. To enable him to get the rations, a small slip of paper was given him, stating name and the amount to which he was entitled, which slip was carried to the Post Commissary who gave out the required quantity.

Issues were generally made once in two weeks. On those days the crowd of applicants would fill the yard in front of the office and enlisted men used to be detailed as guards to keep them back. Frequently I sat from eight o'clock in the morning until seven at night, with the exception of an hour at dinner time, hearing appeals for relief and writing orders for provisions.

Never before had I seen able-bodied Americans beg for food. Among those relieved were broken down merchants, poor school teachers, penniless aristocrats, women whose husbands had been killed in the war, and women whose husbands had deserted them, land owners without seed for their land, poor farmers just struggling for existence, colored women with husbands and without, old "uncles" and "aunties" who could just walk about and whose strength or eye sight had long before been spent in their master's or "missis" service—now turned off upon the charity of the world, and worthless vagabonds both white and black who always begged rather than steal, and stole rather than work.

Among such a mass, it was impossible to be strictly just. Plausible stories were easily manufactured, and were adhered to with all the vehemence of suspected innocence. Sometimes I was morally certain that deliberate lies were told me, but not a word or look would indicate a sense of shame at them. The persons seemed to think that there was a lot of corn and bacon or pork and meal or flour to be given away, and lucky were they who by any means could procure them. It was government property and no one would suffer if they got some of it. I required certificates from at least two respectable (and here I might as well say that I use "respectable" in the Southern sense for a more abused word than this I have never known) persons as to the condition of those applicants not personally known to me. But I soon found that they were easily obtained and were little better than the information I could get from the applicants themselves. Men who complained that unworthy persons were obtaining food would themselves recommend to me others equally unworthy. I thought it a relief when no more provisions were to be had and a great temptation to frequent perjury was removed.

Yet in spite of the tricks and lies that many resorted to, there were many persons who would have died from hunger had not the government furnished this timely relief. Many poor men with wives and children to support were just beginning to start again in the world after their service in the Rebel army, and had planted land enough to produce sufficient food to support them for another year. If they had been obliged to neglect these crops to find work elsewhere for only a few weeks, they would have been total failures.

The people esteemed wealthy had scarcely any money and were carrying on their plantations with borrowed capital, paying for it exorbitant rates of interest. Corn was two dollars a bushel or more and bacon twenty-five cents a pound. A week's work at the current rates of wages could scarcely support a man's family if he were sure of receiving them. It was really a period of universal distress such as I had never dreamed possible in the United States, and at the North where labor is diversified it could not have been possible. One very respectable man—a magistrate—who lived at Windsor thirteen miles distant used to come regularly for food for himself and some of his neighbors. He had suffered serious losses by Sherman's troops, but still had land. He was old and had a helpless and blind wife who required constant attention. Two colored women—formerly his slaves—were the only ones whom he had to cultivate his lands. They had never left him, and he assured me that they had literally supported him and his wife from real kindness and affection. Poor women have walked eighteen or twenty miles and carried home the few pounds of food which they obtained here. One young woman for two or three months walked ten or twelve miles every two weeks to get food for a blind sister. One afternoon on my way down from Edgefield I passed her seven miles from here walking with her basket and bag in order to be here early the following morning.

The land-owners were practically as much in need of food oftentimes as the ordinary poor people. Their land had failed to produce the accustomed harvest, and they had nothing left to rely upon. Their lands, if offered for sale in the market, would not in many instances have found a bidder, and even if they had, ready money could not have been obtained for them. It is not difficult to see why this condition of things should have existed. The people of the South depended on the produce of the land for support after the war was over. During the war they lost everything by the worthlessness of Confederate money and bonds, and by the emancipation of the slaves. Most had, therefore, to begin life anew with only their lands from which to derive benefit. In 1865 labor was unsettled and poor crops was the result. In 1866, the crops failed completely on account of the drought, and in less than three months the home supply of food was exhausted. The cotton which had been raised was sold for good prices in 1865, but the amount realized was soon spent and credit had long ceased to be available in trade. Then too, before the war business had been conducted on the fictitious basis of slave property. Planters owning slaves could readily obtain credit, and were rarely asked to pay their debts. Their notes to their creditors would be renewed from year to year, and as long as their slave property continued to increase, so long were they sure of having money in plenty.

But the war came on and with the blindness of mad men they risked everything with the vain hope of winning at last. But President Lincoln issued on the first of January, 1863 the Proclamation of Freedom, and from that day dates a new era in our National History. Gettysburg was the rock on which the confederacy first struck. There its power was checked and from that day it began to wane. Vicksburg and Port Hudson followed. Grant took charge of the armies and, as I heard my old chief, Maj. Gilbert (now Col.), express it, like a bulldog grabbed the Rebellion by the throat, and never let go his hold until it was powerless at his feet.

As the rebel armies dispersed and as our troops occupied the Southern territory it was found that the people were practically bankrupt and of themselves incapable of sustaining themselves a year. But a stay-law in most of the States prevented the collection of debts, and a partial crop was raised in 1865. But when the terrible drought of 1866 came, a famine was imminent, and hundreds would have starved to death if it had not been for the action of Congress and the charity of Northern people.

Through the Freedmen's Bureau nearly all the supplies which reached the people passed. For its share in thus distributing them it has never received due credit. It has been so much a semi-political organization, its history has not yet been viewed impartially by the Country at large.

I frequently took occasion to impress upon the white people the fact that never before had a government fed from its bounty men who had for years attempted to overthrow it, and who by every law were traitors whose lives were at the mercy of the same government. I do not know as I told them although I often thought so, that they received food one day from the Government or the "Yankees" and cursed both the next.

Since the present Presidential canvass opened, I have had abundant evidence of the correctness of this opinion. I believe that if Wade Hampton and the other Southern leaders who now pretend to be fighting for liberty under the Constitution should undertake another rebellion (which nothing but fear and present weakness prevents them from doing) hundreds of men whose lives and the lives of whose wives and children were literally saved from death by starvation by the charity of the Government, would follow them with the same pertinacity which they showed from 1861–1865.

If misery makes strange bed-fellows, it also makes strange associations. I have seen side by side begging for food the once-wealthy aristocrat and his former slave, and I must acknowledge that I gave to the latter more willingly than to the former.

I will not enter into details of the office work thrown upon Bureau officers by the issue of rations. Any one who wishes an admirable statement of the whole subject will find it most pleasantly told by Maj. [John W.] De Forest (formerly on duty at Greenville in this State) in an article in Harper's Magazine in the summer of 1868 called "Drawing Bureau Rations." His account is not exaggerated in the least, and I think every Bureau officer can thank him for his statement of their common experience.

TABLE I

White Residents of Barnwell County

1867 Months	Men No.	Women No.	Children No.	Total No.	Rations No.	Corn lbs.	Bacon/Pork lbs.
April	20	77	56	153	2450	—	—
May	113	225	486	824	—	28,000	—
June	51	126	257	434	—	11,508	1208
July	52	110	221	383	—	11,270	1726
August	30	103	210	343	—	7728	1764
Total	266	641	1230	2137	2450	58,506	4698

White Residents of Edgefield County

1867 Months	Men No.	Women No.	Children No.	Total No.	Rations No.	Corn lbs.	Bacon/Pork lbs.
April	—	—	—	—	—	—	—
May	—	—	—	—	—	—	—
June	51	116	264	431	—	11,858	1390
July	46	112	190	348	—	10,164	1518
August	10	69	106	185	—	3472	918
Total	107	297	560	964	—	25,494	3826

Aggregate Barnwell & Edgefield Counties
April–Aug. 1867 *

Men No.	Women No.	Children No.	Total No.	Rations No.	Corn lbs.	Bacon/Pork lbs.
373	938	1790	3101	2450	84,000	8524
Average Per Month						
			620.2	490	16,800	1704.8
Amount Issued to Each Person Per Month						
			1	0.79	27.088	2.748
Amount of Corn stated in bushels					1500	

* Issued at Aiken

TABLE II

Black Residents of Barnwell County *

1867 Months	Men No.	Women No.	Children No.	Total No.	Rations No.	Corn lbs.	Bacon/Pork lbs.
April	91	145	58	294	3653	—	—
May	68	92	85	245	2792	—	—
June	66	103	96	265	2305.5	3696	340
July	97	117	153	367	12,584	560	80
August	43	59	24	126	10,943	—	—
Sept.	11	28	8	47	(From supply left from July)		
Total	376	544	424	1344	32,277.5	4256	420

Black Residents of Edgefield County **

1867 Months	Men No.	Women No.	Children No.	Total No.	Rations No.	Corn lbs.	Bacon/Pork lbs.
April	—	—	—	—	—	—	—
May	98	168	144	410	4958	—	—
June	62	129	100	291	1000	—	—
July	60	113	95	268	4000	1344	192
August	20	62	26	108	(From supply left from July)		
Total	240	472	365	1077	9958	1344	192

Aggregate Barnwell & Edgefield Counties, April–August 1867

Men No.	Women No.	Children No.	Total No.	Rations No.	Corn lbs.	Bacon/Pork lbs.
616	1016	789	2421	42,235.5	5600	612
Average Per Month						
			403.5	7039.25	933.33	102
Amount Issued to Each Person Per Month						
			1	17.857	3.445	.252
Amount of corn stated in bushels					100	

* Issued to them at Aiken

** Issued to them at Edgefield C.H.

From the above tables it will be noticed that the percentage of whites who received aid from the Bureau was 56% and that of the blacks 44%. Taking the price of pork at twelve cents per pound and of corn meal at three and one fourth cents per pound the value of the ration consisting of three fourths of a pound of pork and one and one fourth pounds of meal would be thirteen and one sixth cents.

Taking the price of corn at one dollar and fifty cents per bushel and of pork or bacon at fourteen cents per pound (for both were issued and the latter was the most expensive), it will be found that the value of the rations issued to the poor blacks would be $5,752.69. At the same rates, the value of provisions issued to poor whites would be found to be $3,763.39. The aggregate total of all the issues would be $9,516.08.

Besides the issues accounted for above, one hundred and fifty sacks of corn given by the Southern Famine Relief Association were also issued by me. These sacks contained a little more than two bushels each. Nearly all of this was given to whites in the month of June. I think 300 bushels of corn were received from the same source and issued in August and September but I am not positive of this.

The prices used as the basis of the above calculations are much lower than were the market prices at the time. Corn sold readily at two dollars per bushel and bacon at twenty five cents per pound all through the summer. The actual saving to the poor people was therefore considerably more than would appear from the calculations I have made.

Besides these provisions, I received from the Department of Agriculture, Washington a large mail bag containing a bushel and a half of seeds for distribution. They were received too late for planting, but of course everyone wanted some for this year. Many of the seeds were of vegetables that are never raised here, and of the method of cooking which the people are ignorant, and others would be worthless for this year's planting. I think the money used for the purchase of these seeds at the time it was made was of little benefit to the people, although two or three months earlier they would have been of service.

As a matter of political economy, I have no doubt that it was wise in the Government to break through the usual rules and relieve the distress which prevailed here in the South. It is certainly cheaper for a Government to feed a portion of its people who are engaged in raising crops, but who from natural causes have not enough food to keep them from starving, than to allow them to starve and their crops to be destroyed or rendered useless.

I have no doubt but thousands of bushels of corn were raised in the South last year which could not have been raised had not the Government come to the relief of the poor people. Still, the people who were relieved were placed under great obligations to it which they ought never to forget no matter how much tempted to do so by their old political leaders.

Political Condition of the Freedmen

When I first came to Aiken, the political condition of the freedmen was this: they were required to pay poll tax and taxes on property, and to render to the State the same services which were required of white males of the same age but, unlike the latter, they were not allowed to vote or have any voice whatever in political matters. Their condition differed from that of women and persons under guardianship in their having to pay taxes and perform services only required of enfranchised citizens.

In March 1867, however, Congress passed the Reconstruction Act which, by declaring that no legal State government existed in the States lately in Rebellion, provided for the establishment of legal State Governments by the votes of all males of suitable age except a few who were disfranchised for participation in the Rebellion.

From that moment, the political status of the freedmen was of the utmost importance. It would be out of place here to trace the growth of public opinion at the North on this subject or to attempt to analyze the motives of those who carried through this measure. But one may safely infer that it was adopted not from any special love of the blacks or a desire to make up for a long series of oppressions upon them or a belief in their fitness in their then condition for the new duties of citizens.

Except the few old Abolitionists, no one seemed to regard the negroes of the South as of right entitled to the new privilege. But it had become evident by the course pursued by the Southern whites towards the freedmen, from the legislation of the Provisional Governments set up by President Johnson in regard to their civil rights, and from the refusal of the Southern legislatures to adopt the proposed Fourteenth Amendment to the Constitution that the old political leaders, whose influence had not been lessened by the events of the war, were still opposed to the Government, and would not attempt to remodel their states to meet the exigencies of the time. There was too much evidence of the existence of the old rebel and proscriptive spirit and of the irresistible power of mob law to warrant Congress in allowing the ex-rebels to exercise supreme control of the South. No effectual opposition to them could be expected from the few Unionists and Northern men in the South. As a political necessity, the blacks were enfranchised to form a political party which should have loyalty to the Union as its moving spirit.

It was a hazardous experiment to suddenly enfranchise a race which had for so many years been crushed by a tyranny unparalleled in history, but the employment of colored soldiers showed that the instincts of the race were right, and that only opportunity had been wanting for them to prove themselves worthy of the confidence of the country.

As may be supposed, the enfranchisement of the blacks was bitterly opposed here. Even the blacks themselves did not comprehend how tremendous a power had been placed in their hands. Early in May 1867, I think, Sen. [Henry] Wilson of Mass. came here while on a tour through the South, and first addressed the blacks on the subject of their newly acquired rights. But it was two or three months later before any general idea of their political privileges began to be received by the freedmen.

While the necessary action was taken to restore the Southern States to the Union, they were held under military control, Congress having wisely entrusted to the Army the enforcement of the Reconstruction Acts.

Of the actions of the Post Commander at Aiken under the Reconstruction Acts, I have only a general knowledge although I frequently conferred with him relative to the appointment of Registers, etc. On nearly every

Board of Registers and Managers he had colored men appointed, and the elections were conducted quietly and fairly.

On the 19th of June 1867 the Assistant Commissioner issued a circular calling attention to the provisions of the 2nd section of the Act of Congress to continue in force the Freedmen's Bureau, which requires that this Bureau shall aid in making freedmen self supporting citizens of the United States, and making the freedom conferred upon them by emancipation and by the constitutional amendment available to them and beneficial to the Republic. It also directs officers of the Bureau to advise and encourage the registration of the freedmen, and for this purpose to take advantage of the various assemblages of the freedmen.

Here was a new sort of duty required of Army officers but for my part it was not altogether a disagreeable one. The first opportunity which I had of complying with the provisions of the Circular referred to was on the Fourth of July when the colored people of Aiken had a celebration in honor of the date. The weather proved fine, but very warm, and there was a large crowd (many of them whites) gathered to participate in the celebration. In a grove near the village, a stand for speakers was erected and there was the center of attraction. Colored men conducted the whole proceedings which were orderly and pleasant throughout. Two young white men made the first speeches which were in favor of the Democratic Party. They were listened to quietly but their sentiments were very distasteful to the freedmen. One of them made several historical references which were decidedly incorrect, and which were corrected by a young colored man named [Henry E.] Hayne who followed. This man has since been a delegate to the Constitutional Convention and a member of the lower house of the General Assembly.

I made a short speech explaining the nature of the new privileges the colored men had received and the relative positions of the Democratic and the Republican Party. Others followed expressing different views, but it was clear that the freedmen present would act with the party which had emancipated and enfranchised them.

Afterwards I addressed meetings at Hamburg and Edgefield C.H., and had always the ear of the colored people. At Barnwell C.H., Capt. Nuland and I met several of the leading colored men and urged the formation of Union clubs through which the principles of the political parties could be explained to those away from towns where they could be informed of the daily progress of events.

At Edgefield C.H. I had for some time urged upon some of the more intelligent colored people to inaugurate Union Clubs, but they did not feel safe to act alone. I agreed, therefore, to go there and address a meeting if they would appoint one. They did so, and I accordingly rode up there one Saturday in July [that is, July 13, 1867], I think, and found about one thousand colored people gathered in the grove usually used for political purposes. On the outside of the crowd were some whites who had been attracted there by curiosity.

The meeting, like nearly all political meetings of the colored people, was opened with prayer by a colored minister named Harris, and the crowd then sang a hymn. Mr. Ramsay, one of the Associate Judges of the Provost Court, made some remarks and I followed him. Hon. J. [John] E. Bacon was then called upon and made—for a Southern man—a liberal speech. He urged the blacks to obtain education, to be honest and industrious, and not have much to do with politics. The day was showery, and I had to come back to Aiken before the meeting closed. The Edgefield Advertiser spoke of the meeting as quite a satisfactory one.[13]

After that, no further assistance from Bureau officers was needed. Republican clubs were soon formed in which were enrolled nearly all the colored voters. The more intelligent colored men would talk with the more ignorant ones, and impress upon them the necessity for acting in concert with the party to which they were indebted for all the rights they possessed. In this way, assisted by occasional speeches from some educated Republicans, and by the reasoning of a little political tract purporting to be a dialogue between a Republican and a newly enfranchised freedman which was published by the Union Republican Congressional Committee at Washington and which was circulated very extensively, the principles of that Party soon became known and were embraced by nearly every colored voter. When the registration of voters took place, nearly all who could do so registered, and their number both in Edgefield and Barnwell was considerably larger than that of the whites.

In the summer and fall, a very well educated colored man named Eliot [Robert Brown Elliott] made many very effective speeches in both of these districts. From Edgefield he was elected as a member of the Constitutional Convention, and subsequently a member of the Lower House of the General Assembly from Barnwell. While the freedmen were thus active in their efforts to avail themselves of their new rights, the white citizens generally were uncertain as to the course they ought to pursue.

Most who could do so registered but at first were not inclined to vote. Some refused to register on the ground of illegality of the Reconstruction Acts, and a great many were indifferent as to the whole matter. There somehow seemed to prevail a notion that a huge farce was enacting before them, and that they were wise who took no part in it. So they held very few meetings and took no pains to secure the votes of the freedmen. Indeed many men, not in sympathy with the principles of the Republican party, but who were believed to be honorable and just were offered nominations by the freedmen but they refused to accept them. Too late, they awoke to the reality of the change which had been made and tried to avail themselves of some benefits from it.

In August the Registration was made, and on the 19th and 20th of November the first election in South Carolina at which colored men voted took place. It passed off quietly and, owing to the indifference of the whites, a small vote was cast, but it was voted to hold a Convention to frame a Constitution as provided by the Reconstruction Acts.

Of the delegates to this convention from Edgefield, four were colored men and three were whites. Of those from Barnwell, two were white and four were colored. They were not such men, it must be acknowledged, who would be selected for such an important duty in the free states and it may be said, to the credit of the colored men, that few of them sought the positions. But it had been found that the whites who could have been nominated would not run, and those who would have run were disenfranchised. So they were, perforce, compelled to undertake duties which they generally were incompetent for. Still, they showed as members of the Convention good common sense, and helped in the formation of a Constitution scarcely inferior to that of Massachusetts.

When the Constitution had been framed, it had to be submitted to the people for adoption, and State officers were to be chosen. The whites now began to take more active measures to ensure its defeat, not because it was not a good constitution, but because it was the work of a Convention composed of white and colored men and not of the old political leaders. But they accomplished little and at the election, which took place in April, the Constitution was adopted by a large majority, and the Republican candidates for state offices were elected. Gen'l Scott, the Assistant Commissioner of the Freedmen's Bureau in the State, was chosen Governor. This election passed off quietly at the various polling places in the limits of the Post of Aiken.

A third election for County officers was soon ordered. This took place in June and, both in Edgefield and Barnwell, the Republican candidates were elected. At one or two points at this Election, disturbances occurred but no general riot or outbreak took place.

It had been shown by these three elections that when the colored men were organized into political clubs the Republican ticket was successful. The instincts of the colored men were true to loyalty, and could be relied upon in support of the Government. They showed that freedom was a blessing of which they were worthy, and that they would not again be instruments for riveting the chains to their own or others necks.

It would be impossible to attempt a description of the methods pursued by the white citizens generally to oppose the spread of Republican principles and the adoption of a wise and enlightened policy. The arguments of their speakers were mere twaddle about youthful sports, nursing from the same breast, family attachment, and a common destiny. Nothing could more clearly have shown the lack of any effective weapons against the Republicans than the use which was made of such expressions. They must have had more contempt for human nature, more belief in the gullibility of mankind, and more hope in the forgetfulness on the part of the freedmen than people usually publicly proclaim. The freedmen generally showed what, to me, seemed a marvelous willingness to forgive and forget old times. Rarely did those who had been slaves and felt the terrible effects of that institution allude to the terrors of those days. Yet the memory of them was ever present, and easily could a skillful hand have moved to terrible violence those peaceable and affectionate people. I could not but wonder at the temerity of the Democratic speakers in calling up a train of thought which, though agreeable to them who had felt the pleasure of power, could not but have excited very different emotions in the minds of their listeners.

Or if this style of talk—it was not worthy of the name of argument—were not indulged in, there would be appeals to merely selfish motives such as a desire to escape taxation and the burdens of Government. Yet even here they failed, for it was not difficult to show that the taxation of which the whites complained was rendered necessary by the war which freed the slaves. He who had just begun to feel the benefits of his freedom would be indeed ungrateful and unworthy of the blessings which he enjoyed should he complain of the small amount which his labor contributed towards the support of a Government whose power protected them, and without whose aid their labor could never have been their own.

When all else failed, abuse and vituperation were heaped upon the "Yankees," "Carpetbaggers," and "Scalawags" indiscriminately.

Had the Southern white people shown even a slight degree of political sagacity, they might easily have controlled a powerful body of colored voters. Many of them had been kind slave-holders and just men, and were highly esteemed by the colored people. Some had defended their rights before the courts with unusual energy and success. Nearly all had a familiar manner towards them which one not accustomed to the condition of Society here could not easily acquire. They did not need to renounce their old notions in regard to the war or the superiority of the white race to acquire the leadership among the colored voters. They had simply to say, "Although we fought to keep you slaves, you are now free in spite of us and we were whipped. We have now the same interests and duties to occupy our minds. We will make the most of what we could not help, and secure to you by legislation what the Northern people require. Your lives and property shall be secure if you will trust us, and your children shall be educated. At present, you yourselves see that you are incompetent to frame Constitutions and make laws. If you will let us, we will do it for you and do it well." Had they done this, the present condition of things here would have been different. But false pride, fear of public opinion, and loss of social position kept them back, and others won what they could have had for the asking.

I do not know as it would have been better in the end, that they should have done so. There was need of a thorough revolution in the body politic of the South which might not have come except through the presence of a new class of men. It was a terrible ordeal to the proud South Carolina aristocrat boasting of his descent from some noble Huguenot family or an ancient English house, and everywhere asserting his chivalry and respectability, to see the decline of his power and influence and the enactment of laws by men whose positions had been given them by their former slaves.

Still more galling was it to see these measures which led to this state of things carried out fairly and quietly by the military power of a section of our country which they had thought filled with cowards and misers, but which had proved that patriotism and bravery were not extinct in the descendants of those who "fired the shot heard 'round the world" or who fought at Bunker Hill and Lexington.

The teaching of years had led the Southern people to regard themselves as the masters of the country. The North was too busy to discuss idle theories, or to think much about the ugly question which was daily demanding attention. It had come to regard compromise of principles as a convenient way of avoiding trouble, and never heeded the warnings of the old abolitionists or the threats of the Southern leaders. Only when the war was actually before it as a necessity for preserving the national life did it stop to see the reality of the danger which for years had threatened it. Then it sent forth its armies and conquered the rebellion and destroyed slavery, but the old spirit remained, and it is that spirit which is today seeking to again control the destiny of the United States. The loyalty of the North will again assert itself, and time and patience will complete the revolution begun in war and bloodshed.

I write this in the midst of the political excitement which precedes the Presidential election. But it is hardly time to write an account of this canvass. It is of a national character, and every important event connected with it is published from one end of the land to the other. When it is over it may be well to trace the progress of it here.[14]

I have already said enough to show my views of the enfranchisement of the freedmen.

Like others, I had my doubts as to their fitness for the exercise of this boon at the time it was conferred upon them, but I am satisfied that in no other way could the South be properly reconstructed. Everything like caste privileges must be abolished here, and the work of abolition may as well begin now as later. It may be a hard thing for the Southern people to find all of their old notions so ruthlessly disregarded, but in the end it will be the better for it. There is little to be expected from the people themselves at present. New energy must be infused here from the North before the South can hope to assume the position for which nature has fitted her.

As for the blacks, the rapidity with which they have learned their new privileges and duties is wonderful. Where a year ago scarcely one could be found who knew the extent of his privileges, there are now hundreds. Their political meetings which at first were strangely blended with their religious ones—not a bad feature by any means—have become like ours at the North, and are conducted with good order and propriety. By registering, everyone has assumed a surname, and since that time they observe more respect toward each other, generally speaking of each other as Mr. or Mrs. So and So. There seems a little comicality about this, but really it adds to their self-respect and self-reliance and is far from deserving ridicule.

Sam Weller [in Charles Dickens' *Pickwick Papers*] was none the better servant from being called Sam by those whose position towards him gave them that privilege, but he was certainly none the worse for being called Mr. Weller by the "select company of bath footmen" who invited him to the "friendly swarry." But among his equals Sam would no doubt have resented any such liberty as would admit of his being addressed otherwise than as Mr. Weller.

So with the blacks I think it a sign of improvement in the refinements of civilization that among themselves they adopt a more courteous manner than would have been possible while they were slaves. Moreover, their desire for occupying more respectable positions has increased in consequence of the new opportunities which have presented themselves to them, and they have shown a laudable ambition to acquire property and homes of their own and to educate their children.

In fact, their whole lives have been benefited by the exercise of the rights of citizens, and it would now be impossible to deprive them of those rights without a civil war. But such a war they will not inaugurate. They have already suffered without forcible resistance more injuries than most people would, and it will take much to rouse them as a people to act against their old oppressors. All they need now to make them a thriving, orderly class of citizens is protection before the law and freedom from illegal restraints.

With a Republican administration in Washington, this will be practically secured to them.

Rides in Edgefield and Barnwell Districts

As much of my time in 1867 and the early part of 1868 was spent on horseback in going from Aiken to different points within the limits of my jurisdiction, a brief reference to them will not be out of place.

When I first came here, I was little used to horse-back riding, having never learned to ride before coming South. But as the only way of getting about easily was by this method, I soon learned. When Gen'l Runkle was relieved, he transferred to me a horse and equipment belonging to the United States which was used in the performance of official duties.

Before receiving my appointment in the Regular Army, I rode two or three times to Edgefield to attend to some business there, but after my return from my examination in January 1867 such trips were more frequent. Twice I had to go to Barnwell C.H. to distribute rations and clothing before the last of March. Several times, too, I had to go on horse-back to Hamburg, and in the spring of 1867 and that of 1868, I went to the Ridge. The rides themselves were monotonous affairs as I generally went alone and at last unarmed. Until the Reconstruction Acts were passed, I always carried a pistol on my rides, and generally an orderly detailed from Maj. Walker's command accompanied me.

As a description of the country through which I rode may convey some idea of the condition of things here, I will attempt one. I often went from Aiken to Edgefield (a distance of 21 miles) and back in a day.

The soil for the first twelve miles from Aiken is generally sandy. The surface is slightly undulating and for the most part covered with pine woods.

Nine miles from Aiken is a small stream of clear water which flows into Horse Creek. This is the only stream on the road except Turkey Creek, one mile outside of Edgefield. Mile posts are placed along the road. They are of split granite. The houses on this portion of the road are few and far between, and are in many cases mere shanties. Outside of the limits of Aiken there is but one well-built house on the road until within eight miles of Edgefield.

What houses there are, are unpainted and weather stained, and occupied by poor farmers who try to make a subsistence from the sandy soil without the aid of manure. There is one portion of the road about ten miles from Edgefield which extends for about two and one half miles through woods of pine and scrub oak or "black jack" without a fence or clearing. Here scarcely a sound of life is heard unless it be from some adventurous pig in search of "mast" or a hungry cow nibbling the few clusters of grass.

On another road through the same woods is one clearing and one "old field" thrown out for pasture. In the spring these woods are generally set fire to in order that a coarse grass may grow for the cattle to eat.

Twelve miles from Aiken, the soil begins to change. Instead of sand there is the red clay which is more and more free from sand as Edgefield is neared. This soil is better for nearly all sorts of crops, and the houses are better built and more tidy in outward appearance. The fields are under fence and the woods are generally cut down for some distance from the road. Six miles from Edgefield, the road meets the Edgefield and Augusta road. In the summer and in dry weather, this portion of the road is quite good. In old times it was a plank road, and even now, the old boards are seen in many places. In wet weather, and when the planters are hauling cotton to market, the road is dreadful. The clayey soil retains the water, and if many teams pass, a quagmire is quickly formed. The ruts get deeper and deeper, and it is almost impossible to get wagons along.

The roads cannot be mended for fresh dirt would simply make fresh material for more mud.

When the roads are mended, it is in the most superficial way, and the rains soon make sad havoc with them. On hill sides where gullies are formed, pine boughs are generally cut and thrown into them and covered loosely with dirt. These boughs with their close leaves soon catch the washings and make a good road.

After getting into the red-clay country the pines are less frequent and in their place are the hard woods.

In the spring the ride to Edgefield is not disagreeable although lonely enough and without any fine views. Then the deep green of the oak leaves, the fragrant blossoms of the sparkle-berry, and the flowers by the road-side furnish real pleasures to the senses. I do not know how many times I passed over this road on horse-back, but I knew every turn of the road and can even now tell where every mile post is. Except when planters were hauling cotton, it was rarely that I saw people on the road.

I made the journey from Aiken to Barnwell, a distance of 33 miles, on horse-back perhaps five or six times in the year 1867. The soil is generally sandy but towards Barnwell it is mixed with alluvium and the land is consequently richer. The surface is generally level and the road pretty good except where, on gentle ascents, the rains have washed gullies, or where trees have fallen across it and new roads have been cut around them.

From Aiken to Williston the road goes by the side of the railroad which, however, is not fenced. Like the country all about Aiken, it is sandy, and pine forests are plentiful.

Johnson's Turn-Out is the first place that boasts of a "local habitation and a name." Here are three or four unpainted, weather-stained houses generally with wooden shutters and without glass windows and two or three little stores. In front of it is a small pond fed by springs commonly called "Pole-Cat-Pone." Indeed, Johnson's itself is frequently called "Pole-Cat's." Its present name was given by the rail-road officials who established a pump for their engines here. The place is not an attractive one in any respect. Two small houses have been built there within a year.

From Johnson's Turn-Out to Windsor, a distance of 8 miles, three or four houses are passed but the road generally runs through the woods and could scarcely be recognized as a highway. No streams cross it anywhere. Windsor is marked as a town on nearly all maps of South Carolina, but there is not even a turn-out here to give it notoriety.

The town consists of one or two small stores and as many smaller houses, all unpainted and roughly built. The station was for a long time a platform without shelter of any kind, but latterly a shed for the accommodation of passengers has been built.

Soon after leaving here, the road leaves the rail-road for a while and, after passing the fine plantation of Capt. Hightower, goes into the woods again. During Sherman's Raid, twenty three buildings on Capt. Hightower's place were burned. Although a man of property, he has since been living in a log house with but one room. He died, I think, in January of 1868.

When I first went to Barnwell, the road ran across an old field belonging to Capt. Hightower's plantation. Afterwards this was fenced in and the road was changed to enable travellers to go outside of it but lengthening it half a mile or more. It is the custom here when the owner of land has a public road running through it which he wishes discontinued for his own benefit or profit for him to fence it in. He then makes a new road in primitive fashion by cutting down trees and bushes enough to make a new road without so much as asking the leave of anyone. I know several roads thus fenced in to the perplexity of the unsophisticated traveler. Normally, I think, an Act of the General Assembly is necessary to enable one to do this, but practically everyone does as he likes, particularly as there are few fenced enclosures except the cultivated fields.

Three miles from Capt. Hightower's is White Pond. This pond, like that at "Pole Cat," is fed by springs and covers from 50 to 100 acres, I should judge. At times the water is very high, being for a long distance from 2 1/2 to 3 feet on the road. At other times it is quite low, and roads are made which afterwards might be covered with water to the depth of four or five feet. Wild ducks are plentiful here and, in the summer of 1868, I saw an alligator of considerable size swimming after some of them. No houses are near here. Indeed, from Windsor to Williston, a distance of eight miles, no other plantation is passed than Capt. Hightower's.

Williston is quite a village, containing perhaps twenty-five or thirty houses. Here the railroad is met again but is immediately left and is not seen again on one's way to Barnwell C.H. Near White Pond is a small ridge of land which is said by the old farmers to be one which marks the difference in climate between this and the lower part of Barnwell. There does seem to be a difference in the seasons between the places north and south of this ridge, and heavy frosts and snows are seldom noticed below White Pond. The soil begins to be better and more flat, and little ponds are very frequent, forming agreeable rendezvous for wild ducks.

The country is very thinly settled, and woods cover at least half the surface. There is no bridge or creek worth notice in the whole distance between Aiken and Barnwell by this road, and Williston is the only real village on the route. By another road which turns off at White Pond, one has two or three small streams to pass, but on this route there are no villages or settlements although there are one or two large plantations of good land. Over this latter road I never went but once. An Army wagon going to Barnwell with Bureau supplies in the spring of 1867 broke through the only important bridge on this road, and for a long time it remained without being repaired.

Over both of these roads Sherman's troops passed destroying fences, stock and mills, and taking provisions and burning houses. I was told by Capt. Hightower that, after he marched through here there was not a single saw or grist-mill within twenty five miles of him. This being the case, of course, frame houses could not be built and log houses had to be made use of instead. It is impossible to give any idea of the immense amount of property which was destroyed here by our forces. Little sympathy as one may have for the people as a whole for the suffering which they brought on themselves, one cannot but pity the individuals who were compelled to look on and see the accumulations of years dissipated in an instant and thus compelled to start in the world afresh.

The heaps of old bricks and mortar or the solitary chimneys here and there are significant of the thoroughness of the work done by Sherman's troops. Scarcely any of the many features of war which I have seen leave a sadder impression of its horrors than the sight of these ruins which were once the homes of so many happy families.

It was a terrible punishment to inflict on a whole people, but I am not prepared to say it was not a just one. Certainly if the South should again in a fit of madness and led by its old, false, political teachers attempt to resist the authority of the United States, I should not oppose the unsparing use even of the torch.

There seems to be little doubt but the people living in the line of Sherman's march are much more kindly disposed toward the government than those who lived outside of it, although Sherman and [General Hugh Judson] Kilpatrick are hated with all the will of which Southerners are capable.

It is scarcely necessary to make any comments on the condition of this portion of the South as indicated by the above description. In a state which has been settled for two hundred years, with every natural advantage and a delightful climate, one can travel thirty-three miles without going through a single village or seeing a single manufactory of any kind! It is not difficult to discover the reason of this state of things, although the North was wilfully ignorant of it many years and the South will hardly yet admit it.

At Williston, there are one or two small streams to cross but they are not bridged. With the exception of two or three houses built and occupied by negroes since the war, there is no house or cultivated plantation within three miles. The land is low and swampy in many places, but on the upland it is good and could easily be made productive. The distance from Williston to Barnwell C.H. is twelve miles, but I doubt if one passes as many houses as he travels miles on the route. After leaving the sandy pine ridges, the country is less healthy, chills and fever being a common thing every year.

There is a small stream called Turkey Creek which flows into the Salkehatchie River just on the outskirts of Barnwell. The current is quite rapid and the water clear, and when the stream is high it is dangerous to ford it. The bridge which crosses it is badly built and without a railing and persons riding usually prefer to cross by the ford.

The village of Barnwell C.H. is quite small and not very attractive. The first prominent object when one enters the town from the side on which is Turkey Creek is the old Court House in ruins. This was a substantial brick building, two stories in height, with the court room on the second story and the offices beneath. It was destroyed by Sherman's forces, and the ruins are now as they were left by him. The records were sent away on his approach and thus saved. The Court is now held in the Presbyterian Church. A small wooden building, thirty or forty feet behind the Court House, used formerly as a Grand Jury room, escaped the effects of the fire. Opposite the Court House, a block of houses or the jail, I am not sure which, was burned, and further away a Masonic Hall, also of brick, was burned. The churches were not materially injured, and only a few private houses were burned, but nearly all were more or less plundered by our soldiers who were encamped here nearly a week.

Before the war, the place must have been more pleasing in its outward appearance than now. Land is held at a pretty high rate here, town lots selling for one hundred dollars per acre for farming purposes. The soil is quite rich, and two crops can be raised in the course of a year. Wheat sowed in the late fall is harvested in June, and afterwards a crop of corn, cow peas, or sweet potatoes can be raised from the same land with ease. A railroad is graded from this place to Blackville, a distance of ten miles, to connect with the South Carolina Railroad but the war prevented its completion, and now the stock is mostly held by one person who is unable to finish it although the stock was transferred to him for the purpose.

The location of Barnwell C.H. is in an unhealthy spot, and everyone has "the fever" more or less frequently. In the center of the town is an upright sundial of wood which, strange to say, escaped destruction by our troops . [See photograph following page 30.]

The distance from Aiken to Hamburg or Augusta is seventeen miles by the shortest route. There are three roads to Augusta or Hamburg which will require separate description. They may be called for convenience, the upper, lower, and Barnwell roads. The upper and lower road are one for about 3/4 of a mile where they diverge. The upper is quite hilly, and passes through a small settlement of good houses called "Kalmia." I presume the name comes from the quantities of that shrub which grows about here.

After leaving this settlement which is but two miles from Aiken, one rides three miles without seeing a house or a cultivated field or even a rail fence. The road lies though pine woods, and is for a mile or two very sandy. Five miles from Aiken is Graniteville, a manufacturing village of small size.

The village is not incorporated, and the "Graniteville Manufacturing Company" [founded by William Gregg (1800–1867)] owns all the real estate on which are the operatives houses. Horse Creek furnishes the water power, a short canal running from the river to the mill supplying it.[15] The operatives houses are small, but generally well built. The factory is a fine granite building with pleasant grounds, and runs ten thousand spindles in the manufacture of a coarser sort of cotton goods. The operatives are generally white, but are less intelligent than the usual class of operative in the North.

I am not able to give the statistics regarding this mill in detail. It has been in successful operation for several years, not stopping during the war.

Horse Creek which runs near the mill was formerly crossed by a covered bridge, but it was washed away in the summer of 1867 and has not been rebuilt. The ford is quite good except when the water is high, the bottom being of solid rock.

After passing through Graniteville, the road goes again into the woods and only occasionally are farms passed and they have generally a worn out, thriftless look. The road is generally sandy and the country is rolling. The woods on either side are filled with "black-jack" pine and other common trees.

Four or five miles from Hamburg is a small stream which is crossed by a bridge. Near there are one or two brooks which never are high enough to making fording impracticable. From Graniteville to Hamburg, the distance is twelve miles, but no village or settlement of any sort is passed on this upper road.

Hamburg is on the interval of the Savannah River which at this point is about one fourth of a mile wide. Back of the town is a range of hills which afford a fine view of Augusta and the Georgia side. Formerly it was the great slave mart of South Carolina and Georgia. Consequently it was a flourishing place, boasting a bank and several large and well-built houses. Back of the town is an old ditch which once served to drain the sluggish water of a swamp into the Savannah, but now is half filled with dirt and filth.

The banks of the river are so low here that when the river is high from unusual rains, the whole space between the town and the hills back of it is covered with water, and sometimes the first floors of houses and stores are covered also. This was the case in the spring of 1868. In the days of slavery, the town flourished notwithstanding these inconveniences, and many a slave warehouse is now pointed out there where hands were selected for the cotton and sugar fields of Georgia, Alabama, and Mississippi.[16]

Large stores, now vacant or occupied by thriftless negroes, show plainly what was the former condition of the place. Now it has a most wretched, dilapidated look. The wooden buildings are fast going to destruction, and the brick ones look as if they would soon follow suit. On the Main Street which runs at a right angle from the river are a few stores and bar-rooms, and sometimes there is a good deal of business of a small sort done. No doubt the bar-rooms thrive, for they never lack custom either South or North.

As far as I am aware, the character of the people corresponds with the external appearance of the town. With the exception of a few of the old business men, the inhabitants are a lazy, drunken, quarrelsome set, who manage to pick up a living in some way incomprehensible to ordinary observers.

The blacks who congregate here are generally a worthless set who do not follow any regular occupations, and live here because rent is cheap and because they can be near to a city. I know no place where there is so little to encourage one to expect at any future time an intelligent, thrifty population.

From its low situation, it is of course very unhealthy, and there is nothing to induce people of respectability to settle here. As a field for missionary enterprise, it could hardly be surpassed.

The Town Council Chamber is in a low, one story, brick building which is on the main street. Back of the Council Chamber, but under the same roof, is the "calaboose" where petty offenders were confined or slaves were whipped. This calaboose was, when I visited it, without a floor I think, and had over the door a small grating to admit the only light which found entrance to the cell. I left it with a shudder as I thought of the many horrible deeds which had been committed there under a system which Southern Doctors of Divinity had pronounced Christian!

The principal hill back of the town is Shute's, at the foot of which is a lager-beer brewery. This hill was formerly owned by a German of that name, and it is now said that he, many years ago, planted a battery there to bombard Augusta on account of the monopoly by Georgia of the entire bridge which spans the river here. I think it was many years before the controversy between Georgia and South Carolina as to the respective share of the Savannah to which each was entitled was settled.

I have described the upper road from Aiken to Hamburg, and have now to describe the lower and the old Barnwell road.

The lower road leaves the upper a short distance from Aiken, and crosses the railroad about two miles from the village. Here it is quite hilly, but very soon it is quite level and skirts the edge of an old swamp for a mile or more with no clearing on either hand. About three miles from Aiken, quite a stream has to be forded, which once carried a mill, the remains of which are fast falling to pieces. Three miles further on the railroad is again touched at the Graniteville Station. This station is about a mile from the mill and the thickly settled part of the village. Three or four miles further on, the road passes through the village of Kaluna Mills or Hampton.

This village was built by a manufacturing company during and since the war which also built partially a large cotton factory. But through some mismanagement on the part of the directors, the company did not succeed. It proposed to build a large dam across Horse Creek, and made a contract for the purpose, and partially completed it but their funds gave out, and the contractor was compelled to stop work. After the war, the directors raised $150,000 or so in New York on a mortgage, but failing to pay, the whole concern was sold to Langley & Co. of New York, the mortgagees who have incorporated themselves into the Langley Manufacturing Co. Of course, as no machinery had been put into the building, no operatives were there to occupy the houses, and most of them are empty. A suit against this company (Kaluna Mills Co.) was tried before the Provost Court in 1867, and a judgement of a thousand and odd dollars was given against it which it has not yet paid.

The testimony relative to the management of the affairs of the company, which was in every respect Southern and was formed for the purpose of encouraging home industry, was far from showing business capacity and skill on the part of the directors.

Nine or ten miles further on is Hamburg. The road for the most part lies through woods of the usual sort and, three miles from Hamburg crosses Horse Creek, now a formidable stream, and crossed by means of a bridge. (Flat boats come up as far as this bridge for wood and kaolin.) Most of the way from this bridge to Hamburg the country is cleared and several good farms are passed.

The railroad is crossed soon after Horse Creek. In a field by the roadside near the railroad are the remains of an old fort, built evidently in anticipation of the "Yankees." It is an earthwork and was intended for three or four guns and one or two regiments. The "Yankees," however, did not give the defenders of this position a chance to show their bravery.

The soil is better about here, there being less sand and more red clay. Indeed the hills back of Hamburg are of red clay, and in the spring or rainy weather are badly washed and gullied, and the road which goes over them is almost impassible for wagons. Between Horse Creek and Hamburg, two or three hills are crossed, and at the foot of each are small fordable streams.

Between Aiken and Horse Creek there is scarcely one well cultivated, thrifty looking farm, notwithstanding the railroad is close at hand. There are two or three fine plantations between Horse Creek and Hamburg, although a little untidy in consequence of the changes wrought by the war. One of them, Mr. Brook's, is rented out to freedmen and whites in farms of from thirty to one hundred acres.

From Aiken to Hamburg by the Barnwell road, the distance is a little greater than by the other roads; still the road is better and easier for a horse. For the whole distance there is a succession of woods, old fields, and cultivated plantations, all bearing the look of Southern shiftlessness and want of energy.

Twelve miles from Aiken is a small settlement at which is an establishment for making crockery ware from the kaolin which abounds here. I do not know the capacity of the kilns for baking ware nor the number of operatives employed when the manufacture is carried on. Want of funds necessitated the suspension of work here last winter.

The kaolin clay is found in a solid stratum some thirty or forty feet thick fifteen or twenty feet below the surface. It is of a pure white, free from grit, and easily cut. Several new beds have been opened in the vicinity within a year. Large quantities are dried, packed in hogsheads, and shipped to the North, and there it is used for mixing with other clays for manufacturing purposes, adulterating flour or sugar and confectionary. The coarser part of the kaolin makes an excellent fire brick.

At Horse Creek, the road unites with the lower road already described.

The road from Aiken to Columbia I am not familiar with. In the spring of 1867, I went some twenty miles on it to Jones Cross Roads in Lexington District (or County) but cannot pretend to describe it accurately. Suffice it to say, it passes through a hilly sandy country, in many parts very wild, and there are few plantations along it. Not a mill, (I may be wrong here) store, or settlement is passed before reaching Jones's. At the Cross Roads, only one house is found. The telegraph follows this road to Columbia.

The road to the Ridge I have travelled but once. It goes chiefly through the "piney woods country," and is difficult to follow, there being no fences or guide boards. For five or six miles it is identical with the Columbia road, not diverging until some distance beyond Shaw's Creek. This creek is quite deep and in the spring small rafts of lumber are floated down it into the Edisto. It furnishes abundant water power and could drive scores of mill wheels. At present, all its water is wasted. In the same way the Edisto is capable of furnishing splendid mill sites for large manufacturies, but years will probably pass before its waters will be made to serve mankind to any extent. There may be a few saw and grist mills on it now, but they are only for local convenience.

The Ridge is as fine a section of the South as I have seen. For several miles there are well-cultivated farms and many good houses. The general appearance of things is like what one sees in the old free states. This Ridge forms the water shed between the Edisto and Saluda rivers, and rises with a gradual ascent to a sort of table land on which are the fine farms referred to. The soil is good, and capable of producing fine crops. Nearly all the farmers on it are well-to-do, or were before the war. It is twenty five miles from Aiken which, until recently, was the nearest railroad station to it. Now the Columbia and Augusta Railroad passes along it, and will throw it open to the world. There are several creeks near it which can furnish enormous water power. Mr. Elijah Watson told me he had on his place a fine mill site where there was a natural fall of twelve feet. Pine and hard-wood timber is abundant. Nothing but Yankee energy is needed to make that region a most beautiful section of the country. Nature has done her share towards it.

Of the numerous smaller roads about Aiken, it is needless to attempt description. They are generally in bad repair, and pass through the same sort of country which I have been describing. Their bad condition is owing principally to the fact that during the war little attention was paid to their repair as everybody was in the army, and no one felt inclined to attempt an enforcement of the road laws.

Public Men

The most prominent living public men of Edgefield are ex-governors Pickens and [Milledge L.] Bonham, M. [Matthew] C. Butler and M. [Martin] W. Gary, who were Generals (the former a Major and the latter a Brigadier) in the rebel service, and during the last year L. [Leroy] F. Youmans, Esq.

Governor Pickens was Minister to St. Petersburg under [James] Buchanan, and came home while the secession doctrines were first earnestly discussed. He made, as he himself informed me, a Union speech after his return to Edgefield, but the secession tide soon overwhelmed him and he drifted with its current. In those days the Governor was chosen by the

General Assembly, and as Mr. Pickens had been so recently honored by the holding of an important diplomatic office, he was elected Governor and was in office during the eventful days which inaugurated the rebellion.

In December 1860, when Major [Robert] Anderson evacuated Fort Moultrie for Fort Sumter, Governor Pickens sent Majs. [Johnston J.] Pettigrew and [Ellison] Capers of his staff to him to remonstrate against his action as being in violation of the agreement between President Buchanan and the representatives of South Carolina in Congress, that the forts in Charleston harbor should remain in status quo, and called upon him to return to Fort Moultrie or he would be compelled to make him do so. The sequel is a matter of history, Major Anderson positively refusing to return.

The particulars of the carrying of this message I heard told in Anderson in a most interesting way by Maj. (afterwards General) Capers of whose accuracy I have not the least doubt.

Gov. Pickens is now well advanced in years, and devotes his time chiefly to the cultivation of his extensive plantations although, since the close of the war, he has written one or two long and melancholy letters attempting to prove in advance the failure of a free labor system. Personally he is a kind and generous man for whom his old slaves have a great deal of affection, and he was no doubt a very good master.

Gov. Bonham is a younger man, and I think filled the office during the war. He is not a man of great ability although of pleasing manners, and it was his personal popularity which caused his election. He is a violent partisan, bitter in his denunciations of the Republican party and its measures, and unjust towards his opponents in proof of which I have heard the following story from my friend, Mr. Ramsay:

In a conversation on politics one day with Mr. Ramsay, Gov. Bonham complained bitterly of the course pursued by the Republican party and the General Government towards the South, and said no people had ever been so abused and oppressed. As an answer to his aspersions, Mr. Ramsay repeated a few sentences from an address delivered at Edinborough by the Rev. Dr. Gutherie to the effect that the magnanimity of the United States to the South was without a parallel in history, and was most honorable to it.

Gov. Bonham asked who had said those things, and on being told that it was a distinguished Presbyterian divine whose labors on behalf of the poor were a source of national pride, broke out with "He's a G—d-d—d scoundrel and a G—d-d—d Abolitionist."

During the summer of 1868, he wrote a letter to Gov. Scott, saying that the negroes were arming and drilling in Edgefield, and ending with a threat of what would follow if this was not stopped. His alarm had no other foundation than the marching of a crowd of colored people who had been having a barbecue to the house of a Mrs. Bates at her request and for the amusement of her children, under the direction of a man to whom she had given her husband's old uniform coat, he having been a Brigadier General of State Militia.

Messrs. Butler and Gary and Mr. Youmans are practicing lawyers at Edgefield who have good reputations for ability. The last named particularly is a fine lawyer, and is the Solicitor for the Judicial Circuit.

Hon. Geo. D. Tillman's reputation is chiefly local. Before the war, he shot a man named Christian at a gaming table in Edgefield on the slightest provocation. (I have been told by lawyers that Col. Owens, who was the Solicitor that prosecuted Tillman, said that by the evidence Tillman was guilty of murder only the jury would not convict him of anything but manslaughter.) He left the country and I think he was with [William] Walker afterwards on the Nicaragua filibustering expedition. Finally he came home and was tried for murder, but convicted of manslaughter and sentenced to imprisonment for a term of years in Edgefield jail. This he suffered wholly or in part.

After the war he was elected a State Senator from Edgefield District! This office he held when the Reconstruction Acts were passed.

During the past year he has been an active worker for the Democratic Party, and contributed to the Edgefield Advertiser a series of political articles chiefly remarkable for their persistent abuse and misrepresentations of the Republicans. He was one of the recognized organs of the Democratic Party in his County.

Before closing these sketches, it may be well to give a few instances of the sort of teachings which came from the lips of these Southern leaders before the war, derived chiefly from my friend, Mr. Ramsay. Gov. Pickens, one day, at a small country school made a semi-political speech in which he said, "Whom have we to fight against, only those mean Connecticut blue-bucket makers who would run away at the first sound of a gun."

Gov. Bonham before the war, in estimating the chances of Southern success, said that one Southerner would whip ten Yankees, and his opinion was generally concurred in. On all sides the poor Yankees were represented as a mean, cowardly, pusillanimous set who would never stand against the spirited chivalry of the South.

Happily, the war has dispelled those notions.

Edgefield was the home of Preston Brooks, who gained at the South lasting honors for his beating of [Charles] Sumner, of his uncle, Senator [Andrew P.] Butler, of [Louis T.] Wigfall, Waddy Thompson, Senator [James H.] Hammond who made the famous attack on free labor and called the working men "Mud-sills" of society, and many others of greater or lesser note. The mother and a sister of Brooks now live in Edgefield. The children of Senator Hammond now live in Beech Island where they own very large and valuable plantations.

Of the living public men of Barnwell, the most prominent is A. P. [Alfred Proctor] Aldrich, late Judge of the Circuit Court. His father was, I think, originally from Massachusetts. He is personally popular with a large class of people, was a violent secessionist, and said he would drink all the blood that would be shed in the war. He refused to obey the orders of the Military Commander of the District in 1867 relative to drawing juries, and was accordingly deposed by him. He was a delegate to the Democratic convention which nominated Seymour for the Presidency, and was the Canvasser of the Democratic party for his Congressional District. He is a violent States-rights Democrat, and "exiled himself from his native state" by going to Augusta, Georgia after he found he could draw no salary for performing no duties as judge.

Gen'l R. B. Ayers is chiefly known from having been in Congress and being the largest land-holder in the County. The other public men have only a local reputation and need not be mentioned here.

I think there were few men of National reputation from Barnwell. The wealthy and intelligent men generally preferred to look after their large plantations and their slaves to entering upon the "scrub" race of politics.

There are many men there of fine abilities and good nature, and their opposition to the Gov't. has been less of a personal character than in many other places. How much their liberality of views (comparatively speaking) is due to the taste they had of the horrors of war when Sherman's Army ravaged the country it is impossible for me who has come here since the war to tell.

Judge Aldrich's extreme views meet little favor among the majority of thinking people in the County.

Internal Improvements

In Edgefield County there is now building a railroad which runs from Augusta to Columbia. It is expected to be completed this month (Nov. 1868). Through the Southern portion of the County, the South Carolina Railroad passes on its way to Augusta. The former road passes through a fine section of country after leaving Graniteville and getting out of the sandy "piney woods" country, and ought to aid materially in developing the resources of this County. The South Carolina road passes through an uninteresting neglected portion of this County and has but little influence on the improvement of the Country.

The Savannah River for forty miles forms its southwestern boundary, and is navigable for nearly twenty miles by steam boats. Above Hamburg it is navigable by row boats and flat boats. Notwithstanding this long line of river communications, there are no towns or villages on its banks except Hamburg and not a single manufactory of any sort. The tributaries of the Savannah are generally good sized streams and very suitable for rafting. Still, comparatively little lumber is floated down them.

There are no established lines of stages anywhere in the County and no facilities for transportation of travellers or produce except by the railroads mentioned above. In old times, there were plank roads in many portions of the County, but they have fallen to decay, and in winter and spring and after heavy rains the roads above the pine section are almost impassible.

I have been told that many large slave-holders feared to have railroads in the County, and opposed them when projected because the blacks would become restive if they should come in contact with large parties of free laboring white men. No doubt their objections were reasonable, for general intercourse with strangers is not conducive to a preservation of a servile system of labor.

For sixty miles near the north-eastern boundary of Barnwell County runs the South Carolina rail-road, the only rail-road in the County. It has caused many small towns to be built which do a thriving business, and has had a good influence in liberalizing the sentiments of the people. For fifty miles, the Savannah on the other side of the County makes a highway for trade and travel, but only one or two small settlements have been formed near its banks. There are many large streams flowing through the County, but they carry only an occasional saw or grist mill when they might carry factories without number.

No lines of stages run anywhere in the County, nor are there any plank roads. The sandy land prevents the need of such roads as the surplus water which stands on the ground soon disappears.

A rail-road is projected and partially graded from Blackville to Barnwell C.H., a distance of ten miles, but the war prevented its completion and it is doubtful if work on it is ever resumed.

Another railroad is also projected and mostly graded which runs through a considerable portion of the County on its way from Port Royal to Augusta. This road is chiefly owned by Northern men and may one of these days be finished. It runs through a fine section of the County, and would do much towards its development.

The bridges are an important matter to those who are compelled to go far from the railroad, and they are generally miserable affairs. Of course, this is partially due to the poverty of the people who are unable to take proper care of and to rebuild, as they should, the bridges which Sherman's or Wheeler's men destroyed.

In the spring, or when there has been much rain, it is even hazardous to undertake the crossing of many bridges, and particularly those over the Salkehatchie.

It must necessarily be some years before all the repairs needed on the roads and bridges can be completed owing to the poverty of the people, the careless habits induced by slavery and increased by the war, and the lack of public spirit on the part of the prominent citizens of the different neighborhoods.

Resources

What has been said of the resources of Anderson will apply equally to Edgefield and Barnwell Counties. There is some difference in the climate which makes a corresponding difference in the length of the seasons and in the southern part of Barnwell, a few of the productions of the warmer latitudes can be raised to perfection such as the sugar cane and, I think, the orange. Generally, however, corn, cotton and rice with some wheat forms the principal crops. The sugar cane can be raised without difficulty, and on many farms I have seen small lots of it, but it is not relied upon by the planters as a sure crop. Then too, it exhausts the land, and the art of replenishing the soil is not practiced here to any but a limited extent.

This year large crops of rice have been raised in Barnwell County, nearly every farm having one or two acres on it. It is to be hoped that every year the culture of this plant will increase here, as it will lessen the risk the planters will run of a total loss of their grain crops if severe droughts come.

In Edgefield, scarcely anything but corn and cotton are raised. Root crops are almost unknown, and one scarcely ever sees any other winter vegetable here than the turnip which is generally left in the ground all winter.

In the upper part of Edgefield near the Abbeville line, there is some gold, I think, and close to the line in Abbeville, a gold mine is in constant operation. Of the kaolin beds about Aiken I have already spoken.

There is said to be a fine quality of burr-stone about Aiken suitable for grind stones and from the appearance of the rocks in many places, iron ore apparently abounds although I do not know if it is in sufficient quantity to pay for working. The soil is in a large portion of the two counties impregnated with lime, and clay, suitable for bricks is plentiful. At Hamburg and, I think, near Graniteville, there are brick kilns which make a common brick for local use.

A careful application of capital with steady labor could develop profitably all of these resources and improve the country in every respect. Sudden profit could not be expected, but a sure return would no doubt be made to those who enter upon this work after the condition of the country is such as to warrant the introduction of Northern capital and ideas. While there is any doubt of full and equal protection to all men under the law, of course, the South must let its resources lie undeveloped, as its own people have neither the skill nor the capital to develop them.

Under any circumstances, for many years the main reliance of the people must be upon their agricultural resources. The soil will yield generously where properly tilled and cared for, and the climate is such as to render out of door work practicable all the year. The smaller fruits can be cultivated to advantage on the lines of railroads, and wine making could easily be made profitable by those accustomed to it.

About Aiken, strawberries ripen for six or eight weeks beginning about the first of May. Raspberries and blackberries could easily be raised in large quantities and shipped to New York. Peaches grow finely and are very profitable where properly cared for.

Mr. Jo. C. Derby, who bought a peach farm here in 1866–67 raised and sold this year (1868) ten thousand dollars worth of peaches. Of grapes, they sold five thousand dollars worth. Still, the year before (1867) the peach crop was a total failure from natural causes.

Hard work and constant thought are as necessary here for success in farming as at the North or West. The negroes need education like all other classes of people to be good workmen. They can do a large amount of labor, but it is of a superficial sort, and is no better than that done fifty years ago. For success in mechanical pursuits, they would need many years of steady training.

Of course only the common trades absolutely necessary for the comfort of their owners were taught them while they were held in slavery. Of course they were debarred from entering trades which required superior skill and intelligence on the part of the workman.

The effect of this state of things upon the poor whites was what might be expected. They were accustomed to look upon a negro as an inferior being, and would not, if they could help it, enter into competition with him. Nor could they do so profitably, for an owner of a good workman could afford to hire him out at a lower rate of wages than would suffice to support a poor white man and his family. So the latter soon lost his ambition to excel (if he ever had any), ceased to strive for more than a bare support by cultivating old fields upon which he was allowed to settle by the owner, did not pretend to educate his children, and in fact became a poor, spiritless being for whom even the slaves had a contempt. No term of respect was ever used towards them—except when their votes were wanted, or their services were necessary to preserve the system which ground them into the dust—and the phrase "a low-down white man," as used by the better class of people, carried with it nothing but scorn and disgust.

Whatever may have been the immediate effect of the war upon this class of people, and whatever the sufferings their wives and children may have endured while they were fighting for they knew not what, it is certain that it opened to them a new future in which they had glimpses of a new manhood, and experienced hopes of success to which they had long been strangers.

Yet even now, their condition mentally and morally is most deplorable, and it will be a splendid achievement when they are raised to a higher plane of civilization in which self respect shall take the place of abasement, and honest labor of dishonest gains.

The morals of the colored people are of about the same grade wherever I have seen them in the South. Of their devotion to the forms of religious ceremonies, and their outspoken professions of belief, everyone knows either from books or personal observation. But of those deeper principles of morality upon which the welfare of a people, whether spiritually or materially considered, must be based, they may be said to know almost nothing. They have their churches, which they attend regularly; they are ready to give at the call of their minister as far as they can to help church objects; they are zealous in making converts to their faith, and in working effectually all the machinery of ecclesiastical bodies. Still they do not as a class observe those rules of living upon which all civilized societies necessarily lay so much stress.

That this should be the case is not unnatural when one considers the legal barriers which slavery erected to prevent the spread of enlightened ideas of purity and morality. That there are so many colored people who are really good men and women, and whose real Christian virtues have been conspicuous for years, certainly speaks well for their race, and warrants the belief that with increased facilities for education and personal improvement and independence, they can become an intelligent trusty people whose labor no country (and particularly the South) need be ashamed of.

Perhaps through the external observances enjoined on them by their ministers, the way may be opened for the admittance of higher truths and better principles.

I have given above such views as have presented themselves to me in looking back over my service in the Freedmen's Bureau. I have stated nothing for fact which I do not really believe to be so, and have said nothing which can be called exaggeration. There are a few things in connection with duties outside of the regular routine of Bureau work and some general observations which properly belong to another part of this Record.

As far as related to my service as an officer in charge of a District or County, this would end on the 15th of August 1868, when I was designated as Sub-Assistant Commissioner of the Second Sub-District of South Carolina, embracing the Counties of Abbeville, Edgefield, and Barnwell, my headquarters still remaining at Aiken.

Of this part of my service, as well as a few duties I performed as A.A.A.G. for Maj. Walker and as a member of Garrison Courts-Martial and Judge Advocate of a Military Commission, the following pages will treat.

[*End of Part II*

Part III

Duties Performed as Acting Asst. Adjutant General

On the 27th of November, 1866, Capt. Chase, having been honorably discharged from the service of the United States at his own request, was relieved from duty by Major Walker and I was directed to take charge of his district (Barnwell) and also perform the duties of Acting Assistant Adjutant General. The latter duties I continued to perform as long as Major Walker had charge of the sub-district—a period of twenty months. They were not of a difficult character, as at no time were there more than two subordinates under him besides myself, and consisted chiefly in conducting the correspondence of his office, making out his reports, and such other work as necessarily falls upon one holding such a position.

As no clerks were allowed me, I had generally to perform the entire manual labor of his office and my own except in the summer of 1867 when an enlisted man was detailed by him to assist in making out the papers connected with the issue of provisions to the destitute.

Occasionally I made an inspection of the offices of his subordinates at Barnwell C.H. and Abbeville C.H., making a report of the same to him.

The office at Barnwell I frequently visited as the Provost Court was held there and the assistance of Capt. Nuland, the agent, was often of service to it.

Major Walker's district was originally called the Bureau District of Anderson, and embraced within its limits the state districts (subsequently called counties) of Anderson, Abbeville, Edgefield, and Barnwell. This designation it retained until February of 1867 when it was called the Sub District of Anderson. On the 2nd of March, 1867, Anderson and Abbeville were constituted a separate sub district and the name of the sub district in Major Walker's charge was Aiken.

On the 12th of October, 1867, Abbeville was again united to Major Walker's sub district and remained a part of it as long as he remained there.

From the 2nd of December, 1867 to the 1st of January, 1868, the main land of Beaufort District was also part of the sub district of Aiken.

In October, 1867, Mr. C. T. Allen was appointed Agent for Abbeville County, and soon after his assignment to duty I was ordered there by Major Walker to make an inspection of his office. I made the journey by rail and was absent from the office five or six days, one of which, however, I spent at Anderson C.H. with Col. Smith of the 8th Infantry and his family.

Mr. Allen had been a clerk at the Headquarters of the Assistant Commissioner and seemed to be an efficient officer. He had been a Commissary of Subsistence of Volunteers and was a man of a good deal of intelligence. He took active measures to protect the freed people in their rights and for a while did very well indeed.

There was no school for freed children at Abbeville although there were many children there who needed to go to one so Mr. Allen made vigorous efforts to collect money to build a school house and employ a teacher. The people generally, both whites and blacks, contributed a good deal of money (over $200) for this purpose, all of which was entrusted to Mr. Allen. A building for a school was obtained and partially furnished, everything almost being done on it in anticipation of immediate payment from him.

As the price of cotton in 1867 was very low, Mr. Allen prevailed upon many freedmen to entrust their cotton to him and ultimately he shipped for them to factors in Charleston eleven or more bales of cotton. From the freedmen too he collected small sums of money, promising with them to buy provisions at a cheap rate in Charleston for them.

When he had done all these things and borrowed more or less money from merchants in the town, he suddenly went to Charleston, tendered his resignation which was, I think, accepted, and immediately left for the North and parts unknown.

After he had gone, his rascality came to light. Instead of paying for the school house and buying the provisions he had promised, he retained all he had got for those purposes. The cotton entrusted to him he shipped in his own name and drew the money therefor never rendering any account of it. Telegrams were sent to all the large cities in the North to cause his arrest but they failed of their object and it was at last concluded that he had left the country. When I visited his office, he told me he was expecting to make a voyage around the world as soon as he was relieved from duty in the Bureau. No doubt he had then in view the course which he subsequently pursued.

The effect of his conduct was, of course, such as to throw discredit upon the Bureau as a whole, and its influence for good was greatly lessened by his action. Always regarded with dislike by the old slave holders and southern whites, it now became doubly an object of aversion and even a wise administration of its affairs could not, except by slow progress, make its orders respected. The freed people who had been so badly swindled were worse off than before because they could only reason upon its benefits from a personal standpoint and, so doing, they could not but admit the justice of the complaints against it so far as they were concerned.

The bills for work done on the school house were subsequently paid by the Bureau, but, of course, no remedy could be applied to the injuries suffered from the misplaced confidence in Mr. Allen.

Mr. C. C. Perry succeeded Mr. Allen in charge of Abbeville district. He was a native South Carolinian but a Union man, and had never served in the Army. He remained on duty at Abbeville C.H. about one month when he was relieved. Of the effect of his administration I know little.

He was relieved early in February by Mr. O. H. Hart who had formerly been a Captain and Assistant Adjutant General of Volunteers on Gen'l Sickles staff. He was a Brig. Gen'l of Volunteers by brevet. Soon after he took charge of the district, I made by Maj. Walker's order an inspection of his Office. The records had been badly kept by his predecessors and everything was in greater or less confusion so I could not well judge of his efficiency so far as office duty was concerned. His former position as a staff officer led me to form a favorable opinion as to his abilities and I hoped that he could do much to restore that confidence in the officers of the Bureau which through Mr. Allen's misconduct had been lost. He seemed to be earnest in his endeavors to perform properly and fairly the duties of his position.

But I am sorry to say that his course was such as to induce me afterwards to change my opinion of him.

I made a second inspection of Mr. Hart's office in Mar. 1868. This time I made the journey on horseback, taking an orderly from Major Walker's command with me.

I had to be present at Edgefield C.H. at a session of the Provost Court, and immediately after its adjournment I left there for Abbeville. It was the first time I had traveled on horseback north of Edgefield C.H. so that the whole appearance of the country was new to me. The weather was very pleasant indeed, and the first afternoon we made sixteen miles of the forty two before us. As I had left Aiken the same morning, the whole distance ridden was thirty seven miles and besides this I had attended a session of the Provost Court as before stated.

The next day about two o'clock we reached Abbeville C.H. I had thus ample time to make the inspection required and found Mr. Hart's office in pretty good condition and I left it with the impression that he was doing his duty honestly and well, but on this point I could only form a superficial judgement.

The third morning we left Abbeville C.H. to return to Aiken. That day we rode thirty five miles, spending the night at the Broadwater's, nine miles from Edgefield C.H. The following day we reached Aiken about five o'clock in the afternoon. The weather was pleasant and warm all through the trip but it began to rain the night on which we reached here.

The country between Edgefield C.H. and Abbeville C.H. is rolling and the roads were very rough in many places. The soil is clayey, sometimes yellow and sometimes red. In Abbeville the red hills predominate and many of them are without other verdure than straggling tufts of grass which the heavy rains are likely to wash away at any time.

There are ledges of soft rock nearly the whole distance between Edgefield and Abbeville and over them in many places the road passes grinding them down and wearing ruts in them which often become reservoirs of the rain and eventually dangerous slough holes.

Boulders of harder rock are scattered about in many fields and in a few places the ground was nearly white with hard white stones resembling marble.

The soil is generally fertile and susceptible of cultivation and, with attention, could produce fine crops of grain, corn, or cotton.

The pine woods are less frequent after leaving Edgefield C.H. and in their places are woods of deciduous trees. Near the Abbeville line I first noticed the chestnut, and between there and Abbeville C.H. it was quite a common tree and was a good deal used for fence rails.

The farms on this road were more thrifty looking than those about here and many of the houses were fine buildings. The first night from Edgefield I staid at a Mrs. Fuller's who had a very large comfortable house and lived with more comfort than almost any family I had seen in South Carolina. Before the house she had quite a nice flower garden and the whole appearance of the place indicated taste and plenty.

There are many streams flowing in this section of the country between the lines of hills which are so common, some of which could be made available for manufacturing purposes with scarcely any trouble. Like all streams in such a hilly country, they are quick to feel the effects of the rain or droughts and in the winter and spring some are impassable for days in consequence of the rise of their waters.

They frequently sweep away the bridges which span them and from some "penny wise, pound foolish" policy, substantial ones which would be above the highest water mark have not been built.

When I made this trip in March, we crossed streams whose bed was hardly covered by a thin sheet of water but which would after heavy rains have been wide and dangerous streams.

There is of course little use made of this water power and only two or three mills did I see between Edgefield and Abbeville. There are no villages on the route and but two or three small settlements which boast a name. One is Liberty Hill in Edgefield, another is Harrisonville in Abbeville. A mile from the Abbeville line is a public house called Winter Seat but I did not stop there.

On the 30th of May, Mr. Hart was relieved from duty by W. [William] F. DeKnight, late a 1st Lieutenant in the Veteran Reserve Corps. He at once began to make complaints of the violation of military orders by citizens carrying and shooting deadly weapons and called for their punishment. He also represented that an organization of the "Ku Klux Klan" existed there which had sent threatening messages to some of the leading colored men of Abbeville.[17]

In reply to his complaints, he was directed to refer the matters to the civil courts who were required to enforce the military orders of the Commanding General of the military district as they did the state laws.

On his making further complaints of the unwillingness of the civil authorities to take notice of his complaints, in June I was ordered to make another trip to Abbeville and investigate the reports and report on them. This I did and my report corroborated the statements of Mr. DeKnight.

In that report I said among other things—

"On Saturday afternoon in company with Mr. DeKnight, I called upon the district officers and the intendant of the town and received from them assurance that they would do all in their power to secure the arrest of violators of General Order No. 10 of 1867 Headquarters Military District" (the order prohibiting the carrying of deadly weapons) "They all virtually admitted the driving away of Mr. Joiner and other outrages of whites against blacks in other portions of the district."

"I was not altogether pleased with the tone of the local authorities in speaking of the outrages lately committed upon negroes and do not think they can be relied upon for prompt and efficient action except when pressed by the military authorities. As long as military control continues, however, they will need close watching and continual spurring to make them do their duty."

Mr. DeKnight preferred charges and specifications against such persons as the proof he had could convict before a military tribunal for violation of military orders and they would undoubtedly have been arrested and tried had not the new state government gone into operation in a few days, thus taking from the military commanders any further control over these matters.

Mr. DeKnight has, ever since being on duty at Abbeville, done his duty faithfully and well in the midst of much opposition open and covert and often at the risk of his life. Without troops to help him, with a strong political hostility to contend against and subject to innumerable annoyances and insults, he has stuck to his post and faithfully reported all outrages upon the freedmen which came to his notice and has done all in his power for their protection and benefit. He was at one time in a public speech denounced by one D. [David] Wyatt Aiken, the canvasser of the Democratic Party for the Congressional District who said he ought to be hung and one of his reports was called untrue although no proof of the fact was produced nor could it be as he was correct, and his whole stay at Abbeville was full of reasonable anxiety and alarm.

For his firmness and faithfulness, he deserves the highest praise. The presence of his wife and two children at Abbeville of course increased his anxiety. Now that the elections are over he may have a less dangerous, although by no means enviable, position.

These few journeys to Abbeville were the only ones of special interest performed by me by virtue of my position of A.A.A.G. Of the numerous reports which had to be made from time to time it is not necessary to speak as they were much the same from month to month.

The last letter written by me for Maj. Walker was on the 9th of August, 1868, soon after which he was relieved from Bureau duty.

Court Martial Duty

Although not serving with troops and therefore not under the orders of Maj. Walker as Commanding Officer of the Post of Aiken, I frequently sat upon Garrison Courts-Martial in addition to performing the duties of my office.

I was first detailed as a member of a Garrison Court Feb. 23, 1867 but as the order did not specify that Maj. Walker had received permission to detail me on it, I applied to him for information on this point and he accordingly furnished me with a copy of the authority he had received from Gen'l Scott—who was at that time Military Commander of the State as well as Asst. Commissioner of the Bureau—to detail me provided his doing so would not affect the performance of my duties in the Bureau.

I deemed this action on my part necessary as I did not wish to waive any rights which attached to my position by acknowledging the power of Maj. Walker as Post Commander to give me orders. I was not serving in a military capacity under him, and to prevent any subsequent conflict of authority, this was a suitable occasion for bringing up the question. By his applying to Gen'l Scott, he showed that he agreed with me as to the limits of his control and thereafter I never hesitated to obey readily any of his orders detailing me for Court Martial duty. Had he not sought the permission he did, I should have protested against his action and have no doubt that the Commanding General would have sustained me and have treated the organization of the Court as illegal. By reference to my files of special orders, I find that eight times I was detailed as a member of a Garrison Court Martial by Maj. Walker.

This duty, although by no means pleasant, was by no means arduous.

It only required my presence in uniform at the room where the Court Martial was held, generally hearing a plea of guilty from some soldier who had fallen into a military offence through the indiscreet use of liquor and a deliberation on the proper punishment to be inflicted upon him which in no case could exceed a fine equal to one months pay or imprisonment at hard labor for one month.

To constitute a Garrison Court Martial, three officers are necessary, the one lowest in rank acting as Recorder. Its proceedings are held with open doors except when the Court is deliberating. That it was a good thing for the discipline of the troops to have such a court frequently assembled there can be no doubt. The vote of a majority of the members is sufficient to convict and sentence.

The proceedings, after being recorded and signed by the Presiding Officer and the Recorder, are submitted to the Commanding Officer for review and for his approval or disapproval. By him, the proceedings and his orders relative thereto are promulgated to the command in orders. Until that time, the members are sworn not to disclose the vote or opinion of any member of the Court or to divulge the sentence. Indeed, under no circumstances are they to disclose the vote of any member of the Court "unless required to give evidence thereof by a Court of Justice in a due course of law."

Besides serving upon Garrison Courts Martial, I was occasionally detailed as a member of a Board of Survey to investigate losses in subsistence or other stores for which some officer might be responsible.

This duty I never hesitated to perform when asked to do it as I regarded it as a friendly service to the officer calling for the Board.

These were the only strictly military duties which I performed.

Journey to Allendale in Connection with the Martin Murder and Its Incidents

In April 1868, Maj. Walker received a report that one James M. Martin, a white man in charge of the plantation of W. J. Lawton near Allendale, had shot a negro employed on the place, and was almost immediately afterwards shot dead by the other hands on the place while at the nearby house of a Mr. Mallard where he had gone for protection. This deed created great excitement and indignation among the white citizens of the neighborhood which was increased by the report that the parties concerned had refused to be arrested after a coroner's jury had imputed to them the crime.

Capt. Nuland, the Agent at Barnwell C.H., wrote a hasty report of the matter, and went at once to Allendale to see that the law was complied with and that the negroes were properly arrested. In his report he recommended that a detachment of troops be sent at once to the place to assist, if necessary, in preserving the peace.

As the election for State officers and members of the Legislature, and also for the ratification of the new constitution of the State, was to take place in a few days, it appeared particularly necessary that his recommendations should be complied with.

Accordingly, on Sunday afternoon, April 12, Maj. Walker brought to me the report of the murder and told me of his intention to start a detachment off for Allendale in charge of Lt. [Jacob] Almy at once. He requested me to accompany it and investigate the case, and take such action as might be necessary. I willingly acceded to his request, and at once prepared for the trip which would require at least two days as Allendale is twenty miles below Barnwell C.H.

About sunset the troops—eighteen or twenty in all with a wagon for forage and subsistence stores—were ready to move, so Lt. Almy and I joined them and started on our way.

We had to march slowly on account of the wagon and the absence of a moon. About midnight, we halted ten miles from Aiken and bivouacked for the rest of the night. We had supper cooked and then rolled up in our blankets and went to sleep as in the days when serving in the field. It had been a long time since I had slept on the ground in the open air, but I found I had not forgotten entirely the old habits of the field.

Early on Monday morning we started again, and by noon had reached Barnwell C.H. Just before reaching there, the wind suddenly shifted and the air grew cold while a heavy rain began to fall. This continued almost all of that afternoon. At Barnwell C.H. we learned that most of those connected with the murder had been quickly arrested or given themselves up, and were in Barnwell jail awaiting trial. Notwithstanding this fact, we had to go on to Allendale and make the required investigation and if necessary, be there at the opening of the polls the next day.

So in the midst of an almost blinding and very cold rain, we left Barnwell C.H. and marched slowly on our way. About five miles from Barnwell C.H., we had to cross the Salkehatchie River which had been much swollen by recent rains and had overflowed its banks, making what is usually only a swamp a wide stream. The road was a narrow causeway here, and was "corduroyed" and bridged with loose poles or broken and shaky planks. The whole road was under water, but the men and wagon all got safely over it.

After that the road was pretty good for this section of the country, but we were so cold and wet and dismal we did not find much opportunity of admiring the scenery, even if it had been more attractive than it was. At Barnwell C.H. we took into the wagon Mr. Nuland, one of the Managers of elections at Allendale, and Mr. James Just, also a Manager. Afterwards we were overtaken by a Mr. [Robert Brown] Elliott, a colored man who had been a member of the Constitutional Convention who was a candidate for Representative of the General Assembly, and who was going to Allendale to look out for the interests of the Republican Party.

We marched until dark when we halted about thirteen miles or more from Barnwell and six or eight from Allendale, and went into the woods to bivouac. The heavy rain had given way to a "Scotch mist," but after we had built fires and had our supper, we rigged up a rude shelter with one "poncho," putting the other one over us. Under this, Lt. Almy, Mr. Nuland and I got quite a comfortable night's rest in spite of the weather.

Early the next morning (Tuesday), Lt. Almy and I along with the manager of Elections, Mr. Elliott, and four or five men started for Allendale leaving orders for the sergeant and the rest of the men to go back to Barnwell with the wagon. We reached Allendale in good time and found scarcely anyone at the polls. We remained here a short time, and then started for Lawton's plantation and Buford's Bridge.

On our way we met small parties of colored men going towards Allendale to vote, but very few white men. On reaching Lawton's plantation, which is some five miles from Allendale (and here I may as well say that Allendale consists of one store and two or three good houses with perhaps a black smith's shop), we visited Ben Hawkins, the man who had been shot by Martin, and found him lying on the floor of his cabin. He had been shot through the nose, the bullet having cut it and going downwards lodging in the neck. It was a severe (but not a dangerous) wound, for in less than two months he was about his work as usual. He was at Aiken when the Military Commission tried the murderers of Martin.

It appeared that he and Martin had had a falling out concerning the work on the morning of the latter's murder, resulting in Martin getting his pistol and going to Ben's house with it. Ben's wife remonstrated with him for getting so angry, whereupon he struck her or pushed her away with violence. Ben resented this treatment and made some threat or effort to protect himself, whereupon Martin fired his pistol and shot him as stated.

The hands, hearing the shot and guessing its result or being called by someone nearby, came from their work to Ben's house and, seeing what had been done, were of course angry and excited. One of the older men was sent off four miles to another one of Mr. Lawton's plantations for Mr. Lawton or his foreman to come there and see Mr. Martin. However he came back without having been successful in his errand.

The excitement still lasted, and it was finally determined to make Martin a prisoner. He had gone into the large house on the plantation, fearing violence, and as soon as he perceived their purpose he left the house and ran to Mr. Mallard's which was 1/2 mile distant. There the hands followed him two or three of the young men carrying guns. He took refuge in a small building used for a kitchen, and sought Mrs. Mallard's protection, her husband being in the field at work.

Afterwards Mallard came up to the house and tried to induce them not to kill or injure Martin, but to let the law deal with him. Finally, after several attempts had been made to get him, two of the young men, Jacob Green and George Taylor, fired into the window of the house at him, inflicting mortal wounds from which he died in a few hours. A coroner's inquest was held, and about eighteen or twenty men, women, and children were found to be accessories at the fact (principals in the second degree), and warrants for their arrest were accordingly issued by the magistrate. They at first objected to arrest, but afterwards submitted and nearly all were lodged in Barnwell jail.

There they remained until the latter part of May when after reports of their condition had been made and the danger to the health, and even lives, of themselves and other prisoners had been represented to Gen'l Canby with a view to their speedy trial, either before a special term of the Civil Courts or a Military Commission, he ordered a Military Commission to be convened at Aiken for their trial on the 20th of May.

The officers composing the Commission were Maj. [Leicester] Walker, Lt. [Charles B.] Brady, Lt. [Peter V.] Haskin, and Lt. [Jacob] Almy, all of the 5th Cav. and serving here and Lt. Ketchner of the 8th Inf. I was detailed as Judge Advocate.

The charges and specifications were prepared by Col. [Edgar Whetten] Dennis, Judge Advocate of the 2nd Military District, against George Taylor and Jacob Green, the principals. Their trial began on the 25th of May, and lasted four or five days. The prisoners were represented by Rob[er]t Aldrich, Esq., a young lawyer of Barnwell.

After the evidence had all been taken, the prisoners were found guilty of murder and were sentenced to be hung. Two thirds of the members of the Commission concurred in the sentence. A recommendation of clemency was, however, prepared and signed by the members of the Commission, and was forwarded with the Proceedings.

After a careful review of the Proceedings, they were confirmed but the sentence was mitigated to ten years imprisonment at hard labor at Fort Macon, S.C.

Pending the promulgation of the sentence, they were sent to Barnwell Jail for safekeeping, but from there made their escape and are now at large.

It now became necessary to try those who had been found principals in the second degree by the Coroner's Jury. Of these, there were one man and nine women. In their trial, no counsel appeared for them so I had to manage the whole case by virtue of my position as Judge Advocate. The evidence was nearly the same as in the case of George Taylor and Jacob Green, but it had to be all taken down in writing and therefore the case occupied four or five days more. The trial resulted in their acquittal, and they were discharged from custody.

This was the first time that I had ever had so important a case to conduct. As it was one in which great interest was felt by the friends and white neighbors of Martin, I was at considerable pains to read up on the subject of Murder from the standard legal authorities.

It was not pleasant to feel that the lives of two persons, if not more were in a great measure on my hands. Still, there was no avoiding the responsibility, so I did the best I could towards securing the ends of Justice. Technically I had no doubt of their guilt. Still, it would have been hard in view of the provocation which led to the commission of the crime to have had them suffer the extreme penalty of the law.

Throughout the trial, the defendants seemed to understand but little the magnitude of their offence or the punishment that might be in store for them. They made their escape before they knew what their sentence was.

At the October 1868 term of the Court of General Sessions in Barnwell, the Grand Jury in their report referred to the case of these two men, and stated that from information received they believed them to be at large in Beaufort County in the vicinity of Savannah, and that they could be arrested if a suitable reward were offered. The Grand Jury laid particular stress upon the circumstances under which the murder of Martin was committed, as if it added to the magnitude of their offence rather than mitigated it. A copy of their report was furnished me by direction of Judge Platt, the Presiding Judge. I forwarded this report to the Assistant Commissioner with the recommendation that Gov. Scott be requested to require the arrest of the men in question by the State Constabulary force. Whether it has been done or not, I do not know.

A few months after the trial of those who were acquitted, I again had occasion to visit the plantation on which Martin had been foreman, and saw nearly if not quite all of them. It was amusing to notice the cordial greetings with which they welcomed me and the apparent joy they had at seeing me as if I had been their counsel and to me they were indebted for their acquittal, rather than their prosecutor who had done what he could to make out a case against them.

The testimony in these cases as taken down by me at the trial with my arguments, and the General Orders promulgating the findings, etc. are, I think, among my private papers at Providence, R.I.

I have given a brief account of the march of the detachment to Allendale and of the circumstances of the Martin murder, but there was other duty before us in connection with this trip which may as well be described here as elsewhere.

Major Walker wished us to visit as many polling precincts as we could during the election which lasted three days, beginning on the 14th and ending on the 16th of April. Accordingly from Lawton's plantation with the small detachment which we had we went to Buford's Bridge where we found a great many colored and a few white men at the polls, but everything passing off quietly and well. The whites seemed indifferent as to the result, and looked upon the Election as rather a farce than otherwise.

In this portion of Barnwell County, Sherman's forces made their first appearance. The rebel General Wheeler's cavalry undertook to defend the crossings of the Salkehatchie and its swamps, but he was outwitted, and little serious opposition was encountered by our troops. They moved rapidly on to Barnwell, burning a few houses on their way, and seizing nearly all the provisions and stock which could be found. On the large and fine plantations which are there, they met with pretty good success in the way of obtaining supplies.

We left Buford's Bridge about noon and reached Barnwell C.H. about four o'clock after quite an agreeable ride. We were not encumbered with the wagon so, when we chose, could move at a good rate. Buford's Bridge is no larger than Allendale although there are two or three more stores there (but fewer private houses). Between there and Barnwell C.H. there is no village of any kind in a distance of over twenty miles.

At Barnwell C.H. the election was also progressing quietly with scarcely any but the blacks voting. Here we found that the wagon had already passed through, and had gone over the Salkehatchie about three miles from the village. There we went and found the men we had left with it preparing for supper, having built nice fires before our arrival. Here we bivouacked for the night and had quite a comfortable sleep, although about day-light a little rain began to fall.

That day we proposed to visit three polling places but, to give the wagon a chance of taking a shorter road, it was sent one way with a few men while Lt. Almy and I went another with the rest of the men.

The morning was cloudy, but it did not rain when we left our bivouac. We first went to Red Oak Grove, about ten miles from Barnwell C.H. in the direction of the Savannah River. There we found nothing but an old school house or store at a fork of the roads at which voting was going on. There were here but two managers, both of whom were colored men. A few negroes were about the building. The third manager had failed to make his appearance. Everything had passed off quietly the day before, and the greater number of registered voters had cast their ballots, the whites showing their accustomed apathy.

Immediately after leaving here, we descended a steep hill at the foot of which was a deep stream which had at one time carried Patterson's Mill. But the mill was nearly if not wholly destroyed, but whether by Sherman's troops I did not know. Over this stream there was no bridge and the crossing was said to be dangerous, but in we went and got over without trouble.

From here, a ride of eight or ten miles through a sandy, almost uninhabited, section of country brought us to Dunbarton where there was another polling place. It, like Allendale and Buford's Bridge, is nothing but a very small settlement where once there was a store and a Doctor's office. In the Doctor's office the polls were opened. Here too, everything was quiet and the whites as usual staid away from the polls.

Before reaching here, there came up quite a heavy shower which compelled us to take shelter for a time under a gin-house. At Dunbarton too it rained heavily, and there we took shelter for some time. But, the rain not ceasing, we started on again, keeping as dry as we could under our ponchos, and after following a long and devious road whose beginning and ending no one seemed to know, we at last reached about four or five o'clock Tutt & Wilson's store where another poll was open. The managers were Capt. Nuland and two colored men. The polls were opened on the piazza of Tutt & Wilson's store, but scarcely any but colored men voted. Here too, everything passed off quietly, there being no disturbance of any kind.

It rained while we were here, but it soon cleared off enough to allow us to start again, so we again mounted and rode on toward Silverton. The plantations in this portion of Barnwell seemed neater than most we had seen and the land was better. Nearly every plantation was well fenced and appeared to be well cultivated. After going four or five miles, it began to grow dark so we went into the woods to bivouac, the wagon and the other men having joined us in the meantime. Here we spent the night, having a good supper and a pretty good night's sleep. Just before daylight it began to thunder and heavy clouds darkened the sky but no rain fell then.

During the morning, as Lt. Almy and I were sitting over the fire eating our breakfast, we had a call from a Mr. Newman who owned the land on which we were. He had come to complain of the men having used some of his fence rails for fires. He talked with us some time, and finally when Lt. Almy asked him if a dollar would pay for the damages he had sustained and offered him that amount, he declined to receive anything, saying that he only wished to know if we were willing to make good his loss. He further said that if we had gone to his house, he would gladly have furnished us accommodations free of cost and would have sheltered the men in his barn. He talked very smoothly and seemed sincere, and he certainly was the first man I had seen refuse to take pay for damages done by the troops after he had complained of them.

As soon as we had eaten breakfast, we again mounted and started for Silverton, letting the wagon with a small guard take the direct road to Aiken where we were to return that night. There were still some occasional claps of thunder and some pretty sharp flashes of lightning, but we were now so near the Savannah River we hoped the shower would confine itself to the Georgia side. But in this we were disappointed for it soon began to rain; the peals of thunder and the flashes of lightning were almost incessant, and we were in the midst of such a thunder storm as I had scarcely ever seen.

However there was no shelter to be had so we kept on our way until, after some trouble, we found the store at Silverton where the voting was going on. By this time the rain fell in torrents and turned the roads into streams, and overflowed whole fields in every direction. A large stable nearby served to protect for some time the men and horses while Lt. Almy and I visited the polls. The story here was the same as at every other place—everything quiet, and the Republican vote far ahead, very few whites having voted.

We remained here nearly an hour, hoping there would be cessation in the rain and once or twice we thought to start, but a heavier fall of rain would prevent. The shower was all about us, and the lightning must have frequently struck quite near us. Indeed on our way home we saw several pine trees which had felt its effects. Finally we concluded to remount and start on even though the rain was still falling fast. The road in many places was covered for long distances with water to a depth of two or three inches, so it seemed more like the fording of a shallow stream than the moving over a public road. At Silverton we were twenty one or twenty two miles from Aiken, and on our way here we had to visit one more polling place at White Oak Church or some church with a similar name. No one knew the roads, and nearly every person we met gave us different directions.[18]

Finally after many windings and turnings, going at one time around a fence and at another across a field and at scarcely any time in a travelled road, we at last found the church in question situated in the midst of the woods with no house within a quarter of a mile. This was in Edgefield District, the other places we had visited being in Barnwell. It was now noon or past it, and the voting was about over. We saw only one or two vote. They were old white men who could not read, and of course voted the Democratic ticket. Here too, everything had been quiet, and few whites had voted.

The managers were two white and one colored man from Graniteville. They had eaten dinner but had left some corn bread and broiled ham and chicken, which to us who were wet and hungry without any dry food to eat (if indeed we had any at all) looked quite tempting. They offered us these which was all they had, and we were not slow to accept them. We thus had quite a hearty meal, and soon after we had finished it we again mounted and started for Aiken which we supposed to be about twelve miles distant. After some inquiries about roads and an occasional mistake, we finally struck the Barnwell and Augusta road three miles from Aiken at about five o'clock.

The rain was still falling, and every little hollow was turned into a miniature pond whence issued the melodious notes of scores of frogs who seemed as if their happiness at the rain would last forever. Their music had been with us nearly all day, and after we had reached home it seemed to linger about us still.

We got to camp about dark, wet, tired, and hungry and no doubt cross, although the latter feeling soon passed off under the influence of clean clothes, a bright fire, and a good supper.

We had, since leaving home on Sunday night, ridden probably one hundred and seventy five miles, accomplished the object of the journey, and visited eight voting places. It was for me quite a campaign, and but for the rain would not have been disagreeable. A greater part of the journey was through a part of the country new to me, and in that account I was glad to have the opportunity of making it.

It will be noticed that with the exception of Williston and Barnwell C.H., we did not in our journey pass a single village which would be worthy of a name in the North. For miles and miles we would pass through the thick pine woods which seemed never to have been cut, or by large straggling plantations and old fields given up to cattle and pigs without reserve. And yet this was in a fine section of country, and one for which Nature has done all that could be asked!

Views Relative to the Continuance of the Bureau

I have already stated that in the fall of 1866 I recommended that officers serving with troops be detailed for Bureau duty instead of officers on detached service.

My reason for this will appear from the following extract from my Annual Report dated Oct. 20, 1866.

"It is difficult to see why the presence of the lawless men whose conduct has led to this condition of things is allowed in a community in which the civil authorities have full power to arrest and punish them, and the fact that it is allowed and that these men are permitted to roam at large and receive shelter and protection from the citizens shows plainly that the sentiment of the people is bad.

While the landowners and the people who are called respectable shelter and protect these notorious criminals, it will be almost an impossibility to put an end to their outrages or bring them to justice.

During the continuance of this state of things, the General Government through its military power is alone looked to by the freed people for relief.

They cannot have confidence in the citizens when they know that they protect and sympathize with murderers, robbers, and incendiaries and they naturally appeal to officers of this Bureau for protection. To remove entirely these officers and the military forces would be to deprive them of every chance of protection and expose them to greater outrages and more villainy.

There should, it seems to me, be evidences of a change of sentiment among the white citizens before the United States can safely give up its control of the freedmen.

It may not be necessary to have an officer especially charged with looking after the interests of the freedmen after this year as the military commanders of Posts could do this, but that they should be protected in their rights by the military power if necessary is only too apparent.

I would therefore recommend that the duties now required from Officers of this Bureau be performed by military commanders whenever the civil authorities show even a partial willingness to take cognizance of cases referred to them by the freed people."

At the time this report was made, the powers of Bureau officers were very limited inasmuch as all cases to which they were parties had to be referred to the Civil courts.

Only by an almost arbitrary and, consequently, dangerous stretch of his authority could a Bureau officer interfere to protect the rights of the freedmen. There seemed then, no probability of the military authorities again being entrusted with the supervision of the whole machinery of government in the rebellious states. Therefore it did not appear to me well to keep in pay a large body of officers performing nominal duties but without any real power or influence. They had to rely entirely on the Post Commanders for cooperation and support and upon the latter all responsibility virtually rested.

Where they were not required to make specific reports of their action, it was almost impossible that there should not arise causes of difference between them and Bureau officers. By the removal of the latter, the entire responsibility would fall upon Post Commanders—where it belonged—and the freedmen would consequently be more likely to be protected by the military authorities.

But after the passage of the Reconstruction Acts, the Post Commanders in the Military Districts were detailed as Bureau Officers as well so the inconveniences and jealousies arising from a double-headed system were avoided and everything worked smoothly as far as I am aware. Even before the passage of the Reconstruction Acts, Maj. Walker had been detailed for duty in the Bureau in addition to his other duties.

In December 1867, a report was called for based upon observations of Bureau Officers in regard to the necessity of continuing the Freedmen's Bureau beyond the time fixed by law for its discontinuance (July 16, 1868).

My views on this subject were stated in part as follows in my report dated Dec. 29, 1867.

"There is of course much advantage in having an officer to advise and, as far as possible, look after the interests of the freedmen of the different districts but now that the colored men have been endowed with the same political and civil rights as the whites, it is a question whether they ought longer to be subjects for special legislation.

With the ballot in their hands, having a voice in choosing the officers of the state and of their district, and in making laws, it seems to me that they should not look longer to the General Government for assistance. It will, of course, depend chiefly on the course of the people in regard to the new Constitution for the State which will probably be formed, whether it is necessary for the Military authorities to be supreme in this State. But if the terms prescribed by the Government are complied with, and loyal and republican State governments are established, the people should themselves manage their own affairs and should appeal to their own officers for protection and redress of grievances."

"The business of Bureau officers between now and July, 1868 will be chiefly confined to settling accounts between freedmen and employers for work done this year (1867), approving contracts for 1868, and settling little disputes which may from time to time be referred to them. If before next July, the civil government of the State is established, I can see no reason why the Bureau should [not] be discontinued. There must, of course, be a military force in the State for some time to come to assist in enforcing the laws and maintaining peace and good order, and if the freedmen are thought to need protection on account of their ignorance of the rights and privileges of citizens, it could be furnished by the military authorities.

It seems to me that it is time that the people, white as well as black, should rely upon themselves in all that pertains to the machinery of Government. There will be much suffering, perhaps some bloodshed and disturbance, before such communities as exist in the old free States can be established, but in the end it will be better for the people to learn self-government in this way than to be accustomed and indifferent to a state of martial law.

It has been shown conclusively during the past year that law and order can be maintained where officers are not afraid of criminals and where the ends of justice rather than personal popularity are sought.

With a new code of laws which will enable anyone to secure his just rights without unnecessary expense or delay, with judges whose office does not depend upon the uncertainty of popular favor, with intelligent juries and the means of education within the reach of all, the future destiny of the colored people can, without fear, be left to themselves."

"Peace and security for person and property are essential to the development of the resources of the Country and the improvement of the people. If the civil law will not provide for this the military law must.

At present I see no reason why the Reconstruction measures which Congress has adopted should not accomplish the results anticipated from them.

With this belief, I cannot see the necessity for continuing the Freedmen's Bureau beyond the time now directed by law. Should the people of the State, however, defeat the measures for restoring it to its proper relation to the General Government, I think it would be absolutely necessary that the Bureau should be continued and that its authority be extended to enable its officers to hold courts for the settlement of all controversies arising from breaches of contracts to which freedmen are parties."

I think that subsequent events have justified the opinions expressed in the quotations above made.

The people of this state ratified the Constitution made by the Convention convened by virtue of the Reconstruction Acts and elected a loyal State Government which was duly inaugurated and to which, and the authorities under it, were formally relinquished by Gen'l Canby, the District Commander, on the 24th of July, 1868 all powers before exercised by him over the civil affairs of the people.

There has been, to be sure, something to do since that time by Bureau officers but they have been utterly powerless to take efficient measures to protect or vindicate the rights of the freedmen. It was no doubt well in view of the uncertainty of the course of events in the South to be prepared for the worst and consequently to continue the Bureau wherever the Commissioners might deem the presence of its officers necessary but, apart from its continuance as a precautionary measure, its longer existence in the reconstructed States would have been of little practical use except so far as the educational and bounty-collecting branches are concerned.

I think under no circumstances would it have been well to retain in the pay of the Government a class of officers whose position gave them little or no influence merely for the sake of reporting from time to time the results of their observations. When the Government bestowed on the colored people the right of suffrage, it could no longer treat them as wards requiring aid and protection, but as citizens acquainted with their rights and able to maintain them in the ordinary, legal way. Certainly nothing like military influence could afterwards be allowed either in their favor or against them except when exerted at the request of the proper civil authorities.

Loans of Provisions Made to Planters

In consequence of the almost total destruction of the crops of cotton on the sea islands and of the rice in the lower section of the State, there appeared to be no way for another attempt to retrieve their fortunes except by the planters receiving advances of supplies from the General Government through Gen'l Scott, the Assistant Commissioner of the Bureau. He was accordingly authorized to make advances to responsible persons of corn and bacon for which the planters gave a lien on their crops for the value of the same to be paid from the first proceeds of their sales. This relief was intended chiefly for the "low country" as in the upper Districts good crops of corn had been made and there was little or no danger of suffering from want of food.

Gen'l Canby issued an order making the lien of Gen'l Scott in behalf of the United States prior to all liens and claims of any kind whatsoever except such as might have or might be entitled to priority under any act of Congress and making it cover the crop and personal and real estate of the person receiving the advances. The order further provided that if any person should remove, conceal, dispose of, destroy, or injure any property subject to this lien, he should be liable to the penalties provided by law for larceny. The General Assembly of the State at its Special Session passed a law re-enacting this order, thus effectually guarding the rights of the United States.

Early in the season one or two applications from planters in the Edgefield District were made to the Assistant Commissioner for advances of provisions but as they were not favorably considered at once they were not pressed and no issues were made. Later in the season—that is in June and the early part of July—a few applications were made by persons near Hamburg which, after much hesitation, I forwarded approved. But the amount required was so small, the Assistant Commissioner declined to furnish it.

In my monthly report for May, 1868 dated June 1, I referred to the issue of provisions to planters in these words—

"Some of those (freedmen) who rented land are now pressed for provisions but none have been sent me for distribution. Indeed, I think it would not be advisable to make loans of provisions in my District (Edgefield). If they are made this year, many will rent land expecting similar assistance next year and if they fail to receive it, will necessarily lose their work and their crops.

There is no way in which the majority of freedmen will learn but by experience.

Many have thought that if they could get land they could raise crops, even if they had neither supplies nor animals. As soon as the hot weather comes, and the work is pressing, they find themselves without provisions and without money. If they could have applied reason to their affairs they would have seen that failure was inevitable and would have waited a year or two before trying to carry on places of their own.

But, if when some are hard pressed this year and, instead of receiving assistance from the Government, are compelled to lose their crops, while it will be hard for individuals, it will be better for the community at large. Both the whites and the blacks must learn to rely wholly on themselves and each other and the less they receive from the Bureau, as a rule, the better it will be for them."

So again in my report dated July 1st, I said—

"I have forwarded an estimate of provisions which are required for issue on liens in the vicinity of Hamburg but none have thus far been sent me. It is now so late in the season, it is doubtful if issues made now would be of service and it certainly would be better if crops could be raised without them.

It will be a hard lesson for many freedmen who have endeavored to raise crops on rented land with insufficient means but in the end it will be better for them. If issues on liens are made now, no amount of assertion that provisions will not be loaned next year by the United States can prevent freedmen from attempting to carry on farms of their own next year without having the necessary provisions to carry them through these months. They will know that the Government has relieved some this year and will believe that similar relief will be afforded next year.

While this office has always encouraged the hiring or purchase of farms by industrious freedmen who had sufficient means to carry them on successfully, it has discouraged the idea many freedmen seem to have that a piece of land and an old, broken down horse are sufficient to ensure them not only subsistence while raising a crop but abundance for the next year.

No freedman—nor in fact, any person—should, without having credit, attempt to carry on a farm unless he has six months' provisions to start with for, if he does, failure is certain and the effects of such failure are felt not only by the man himself but by the whole community."

Had there been such a failure in the crops in Edgefield District as there was on the Sea Islands, I probably should have looked with greater favor on the scheme of relieving planters by means of loans of provisions. But it was generally said that the corn crop of Edgefield was greater than it had been for years, so I did not think it well to import corn where there was more than enough at home to supply the demand.

So no provisions whatever were loaned in that District, and this source of trouble and anxiety was saved me. In Barnwell District, C[harles] P. Leslie, a member of the Constitutional Convention and subsequently State Senator from that District did succeed in getting Gen'l Scott to send to him at Blackville some three hundred bushels of corn and eighteen hundred pounds of bacon to be loaned to planters. This he issued wholly or in part before Capt. Nuland received any information regarding these supplies. It was Leslie's duty to see that all persons to whom he made these advances signed a bond to pay for them, but in many instances he failed to do this. While I do not think for a moment that Gen'l Scott—who was then a candidate for Governor of the State and was subsequently elected to that office—intended that these supplies should be given as a bribe to induce any people to vote for him, I do believe that Leslie got them really for the purpose of acquiring popularity and strengthening himself in his political schemes. At any rate, he ceased to take any pains to protect the interests of the United States after he received the supplies and he had been elected to the Office which he was seeking. From many of those to whom he issued—himself included—it will be impossible ever to get one cent in payment of their indebtedness.

As soon as his consignment was exhausted, Capt. Nuland was beset by hundreds of applicants and could not avoid applying for more which was duly furnished. So between Leslie and him there were in all sent to Barnwell and issued two thousand and fifty (2050) bushels of corn and ten thousand (10,000) pounds of bacon. Besides these amounts, there were issued to four planters directly from the Headquarters Assistant Commissioner, three hundred and ninety eight (398) bushels of corn and two thousand three hundred and eighty eight (2388) pounds of bacon.

These supplies were issued to forty four whites and eighty six blacks and amounted in value to five thousand seven hundred and eight dollars and thirty cents ($5708.30), the value of those issued to whites being three thousand six hundred and two dollars and forty three cents ($3602.43) and of those issued to freedmen two thousand one hundred and five dollars and seventeen cents ($2105.17).

The gross price of corn was one dollar and fifty one cents ($1.51) per bushel and of bacon sixteen and three fourths cents ($.16 3/4) per pound.

On the 28th of September I was ordered to assume charge of the collection of bonds given for these supplies, but of this duty more will be said hereafter.

Although many persons were materially aided by these loans and were enabled to carry on plantations which they could not have done without them, many received supplies who did not need them and were not entitled to them.

Duties Performed as Sub-Assistant Commissioner

On the 17th of August, 1868, in accordance with Par.2, General Orders No. 7, Headquarters Assistant Commissioner, I assumed charge of the Second Sub-District of South Carolina embracing the counties of Abbeville, Edgefield, and Barnwell.

I had previously (on the 10th of July) made application for a leave of absence for two months with permission to apply for an extension of three months as I did not think there would be any important work for me to do after the State government was fairly in operation and I had had no leave for five years.

But as I received a letter from the Headquarters Assistant Commissioner dated July 18 in which it was stated that, "in view of a probable reorganization of the Bureau in this State for the short period now remaining of its existence, he desires your services having in view your assignment as Sub-Assistant Commissioner to one of some seven or eight Districts into which the state will be divided for a more systematic administration of affairs," I concluded to withdraw my application temporarily.

I had one officer under me—Mr. W. F. DeKnight—who was in charge of Abbeville County. To me he made all his reports and received his instructions.

As soon as possible after assuming charge of the Sub-District, I paid a visit to Abbeville to inspect the condition of his office and see how things were going on there. The office I found in good condition and Mr. De-Knight was performing his duties with great faithfulness and ability.

On my way to Abbeville, I had to stop at Columbia and there for the first time since being on duty in the State visited the Headquarters of the Assistant Commissioner which had but a few days before been removed to that place from Charleston. Bvt. Col. J[ohn] R. Edie, Lt. Col. 8th Infantry, had relieved General Scott as Assistant Commissioner upon the inauguration of the latter as Governor of the State. I had a few minutes conversation with him and became acquainted with the staff officers, none of whom but Maj. [Erastus] Everson had I previously seen.

After having made this journey to Abbeville, I made one to Allendale and sent reports of both to the Assistant Commissioner.

My work had not been much increased by my assignment to a larger extent of territory for, as before stated, the power of Bureau officers in the way of affording palpable relief and protection to the freedmen ceased when the new State Government was inaugurated.

But when I had thrown upon me the duty of collecting the payment for the supplies issued by Capt. Nuland, my work was much increased.

The first thing to be done was to make out an elaborate report showing the name, color and residence of every person who received supplies from the Government, the amount of corn or bacon received by each and the net price of the same, the cost of transportation and drayage to be added to each account, and the total value to be charged to each.

To do this I made a journey to Barnwell C.H. and obtained from Capt. Nuland such bonds as he had and a list of the issues but the other data he was unable to furnish nor could they be had except at Headquarters in Columbia. So there I went at once and found my friend, Maj. Everson who had been put in charge of the whole business and who was hard at work consolidating the reports of other officers.

From him I obtained the desired information and in the day I spent at Columbia half-finished the report. But it was not completed until my return to Aiken and there a copy had to be made of it.

This done, I went to work immediately to collect. I first sought and obtained permission to hire a messenger to carry notices to those who had received supplies to send their produce to certain merchants in the villages nearest them or to meet me at their stores to pay in currency their indebtedness. The notices were printed for me at Headquarters. Then I visited the places where the greater number of those who owed lived (Blackville and Barnwell C.H.) and collected as much as I could. There were many complaints made that the full amount of supplies charged were not received and some grumbling at the price but for neither of these was there any help. Very few paid up on the first demand, pleading the impossibility of getting their cotton ginned and sent to market, others of inability to collect debts, and others were under the impression that the supplies would not have to be paid for at all.

In the month of October I succeeded in collecting four hundred and twenty seven dollars and forty nine cents, ($427.49).

In November I collected one thousand nine hundred and eighty seven dollars and sixty seven cents ($1987.67). The collections for the present month (December) are not yet completed but I have been compelled to place the claims against about forty persons in the hands of the Sheriff for collection. From many of them I fear it will be impossible to realize anything.

Notes to the Record of Service

The editors have made every effort to ensure a faithful rendering of the 140-year-old handwritten record of his service in the Freedman's Bureau exactly as William Stone wrote it. In doing so, we have resisted the temptation to modernize his spelling and punctuation or to correct slight differences in names and numbers. Even the titles and numbering of the parts are Stone's own.

1. At the time one could reach Mt. Pleasant from Charleston only by boat.

2. The "Swamp Angel" was a massive Parrott cannon placed on a wood platform in a swampy area opposite Charleston in 1863. It owed its nickname to the army engineers who hauled it in place to bombard the city into submission. Its two-hundred-pound incendiary shells rained death and destruction on the city for two days before it blew itself up on its thirty-sixth shot.

3. Stone's dates for his stay in Charleston are confused. By his own report, he arrived there March 12 (p. 1), stayed "a week" until March 17 (p. 3), and left on March 16 (p. 4).

4. Most reports agree that copious quantities of liquor "liberated" by the rampaging Union troops combined with the bales of flammable cotton piled in the streets by retreating Confederates made for a highly incendiary mixture.

5. Prior to this time Stone had no legal training whatsoever. Within three years of writing this, he had qualified to practice law in South Carolina and was a partner in a Charleston law firm. Five years after that he became attorney general of South Carolina.

6. Britain unilaterally outlawed the slave trade in 1807. Interestingly enough Article I, Section 9, of the U.S. Constitution specifically enjoined Congress from prohibiting the foreign slave trade before the year 1808. Then, in the Webster-Ashburton Treaty of 1842, the United States and Great Britain agreed that they would "urge upon all powers the propriety and duty of closing such [slave] markets effectually at once and forever."

7. These were the so-called Black Codes adopted by many of the former states of the Confederacy (including South Carolina) in an attempt to suppress any possibility of equality between freed slaves and whites. They aroused vigorous indignation in the North and were promptly overturned by military authorities and Congressional legislation.

8. Throughout his report, Major Stone exhibits a strong interest in the agricultural methods and resources of the South, reflecting his own youthful years on his family's farm in Massachusetts.

9. Possibly Stone is referring here to Shakespeare's play *The Tempest* in which the "savage and deformed slave" Caliban is described as a "brutish" member of a "vile race" (I.ii).

10. Stone's frequent references to railroads in the narrative reflect the importance of that mode of travel and transportation in post–Civil War America.

11. Edgefield, South Carolina, has a long and well-earned reputation for violent behavior and blood feuds, both intra- and interracial. Numerous placards and historical markers posted downtown describe various murders and shoot-outs that have occurred on the village green.

12. In December 1868, as Stone was finishing this report, Martha Schofield, a Quaker from Pennsylvania, arrived in Aiken and established, with his help, a school for black children. Today it is a highly regarded middle school with a magnificent modern campus. It was finally racially integrated in 1970.

13. In a report of this meeting titled "Mass Meeting of Freedmen," the *Edgefield Advertiser* of July 17, 1867, quoted Major Stone at length, including his interesting warning about charlatans: "The Freedmen should not be deterred from the Registration or ballot box by artful men with threats of having to pay money for the privilege—one dollar or more before registering; there was nothing in this."

14. Major Stone never did return in this narrative to the subject of the national election of 1868, which saw Ulysses S. Grant, the Republican, triumph over Democrat Horatio Seymour to become the nation's president. The campaign was marked by a Ku Klux Klan–instigated reign of terror against blacks and white Republicans throughout the South.

15. The mill, which opened in 1845, was closed in 2006 following a catastrophic train derailment in 2005 that killed 9 people, injured 250, and seriously damaged the plant (*State,* July 19, 2006).

16. One of these old warehouses played a prominent, and tragic, role in the Hamburg massacre of July 1876.

17. This is Stone's first reference to the Ku Klux Klan, which was just beginning its deadly rampage through the entire South that culminated in South Carolina with the Ku Klux Klan trials of 1871–72.

18. Many of the towns identified by Major Stone in his report no longer exist because they were located in an area appropriated by the federal government in the mid–twentieth century for a nuclear weapons program named the Savannah River Plant project.

Index

About the Editors

The great-granddaughter of William Stone, Suzanne Stone Johnson is a retired schoolteacher and coeditor of her community newspaper in Leesville, South Carolina. She earned her B.S. degree from Tufts University, certification as an occupational therapist from the Boston School of Occupational Therapy, and an M.Ed. degree from American International College in Springfield, Massachusetts.

Robert Allison Johnson is the author of *This Violent Land,* a historical novel based on the life of William Stone. He is a retired insurance professional with a B.A. degree in history from Harvard University and an M.B.A. from Western New England College.